Captain James Cook

THE WORLD'S GREAT EXPLORERS

James Cook

By Zachary Kent

Consultant:
Dr. James Casada, Ph.D., Professor of History,
Winthrop College, Rock Hill, South Carolina

CHILDRENS PRESS ®
CHICAGO

James Cook's house—now in Fitzroy Gardens, Melbourne, Australia—was brought there from Yorkshire, England, and reassembled.

Project Editor: Ann Heinrichs
Designer: Lindaanne Donohoe
Cover Art: Steven Gaston Dobson
Engraver: Liberty Photoengraving

**Library of Congress
Cataloging-in-Publication Data**

Kent, Zachary.
  James Cook / by Zachary Kent.
    p. cm. — (The World's great explorers)
    Includes bibliographical references and index.
    Summary: The life of the British navigator
and explorer whose three famous voyages
resulted in the accurate mapping of much of the
South Pacific.
    ISBN 0-516-03066-3
    1. Cook, James, 1728-1779—Juvenile litera-
ture. 2. Explorers—Great Britain—Biography—
Juvenile literature. [1. Cook, James, 1728-1779.
2. Explorers.] I. Title. II. Series.
G246.C6K46 1991   91-12571
910'.92—dc20   CIP
[B]   AC

Statue of James Cook in Victoria, British Columbia

Table of Contents

Chapter 1
Kealakekua Bay

Gusts of wind pitched two small British ships across the great, green Pacific Ocean. Hard months at sea had left the *Resolution* and the *Discovery* in cruelly battered condition. Creaking masts threatened to topple, ropes were split and frayed, and whistling breezes showed where sails were torn. Out of the icy waters of the North Pacific the ships sailed south in search of a safe harbor. Captain James Cook, commander of this exploring expedition, had discovered and briefly visited the Hawaiian Islands the year before. Now he decided they would be the best place to rest his crews and make repairs.

Day after day barefoot sailors tiredly climbed into the ships' rigging and scanned the horizon. Finally, on January 17, 1779, an opening appeared on the western coast of Hawaii, the largest island in the group. The ships coasted forward into Kealakekua Bay, and a quarter mile (.4 kilometer) from shore Captain Cook ordered sails furled and anchors dropped.

The tropical sun and the lush green hills warmed the spirits of the exhausted crews. But the surprising welcome of the Hawaiian natives filled them with even greater joy. In hundreds of carved wooden canoes, smiling islanders paddled across the water and surrounded the two ships. "I have nowhere in this sea seen such a number of people assembled in one place," Cook later exclaimed. "Besides those in the canoes, all the shore of the bay was covered with people, and hundreds were swimming about the ships like shoals of fish." As many as ten thousand people filled the waters and beaches of the bay.

Golden-skinned Hawaiians climbed aboard the British ships. Women hung wreaths of bright and fragrant flowers around the sailors' necks. Islanders cheerfully danced and sang on the crowded decks. From their canoes they lifted aboard wooden bowls brimming with delicious fruits, coconuts, and vegetables. Bowing low, natives presented the strangers with roast pigs wrapped in palm leaves. Overwhelmed by these unexpected celebrations, the British seamen imagined they had entered paradise.

In these delightful surroundings Captain Cook put his crew to work. During the next days the sailors caulked leaks and ships' carpenters hammered repairs on masts and planking. Nimble fingers stitched patches on sails and spliced new ropes. Shore parties filled barrels with fresh water and collected bundles of firewood. With unusual friendliness, the Hawaiians supplied the crewmen with constant gifts of food.

The natives especially showed fifty-year-old Captain Cook the greatest possible respect whenever he stepped ashore. As he walked among the grass huts of their village, they dropped to their knees and bowed.

Captain Cook landing in Hawaii

Island chiefs presented him with feathered helmets and beautiful red-feather robes. Native priests followed behind him everywhere and solemnly called him "Rono."

Cook hardly understood the meaning of it all. In a spirit of friendship, he agreed to take part in elaborate rituals. Koa, the high priest, led him up the ramp of a stone platform. Human skulls grinned from the posts of the railing. Inside a wooden chamber at the top of the platform stood large, carved religious idols. With grave ceremony, Koa and a priest named Kili'ikea draped a red cloth about Cook's shoulders. Servants carried in dead and living pigs, while the two priests chanted. Then Kili'ikea rubbed Cook's face, head, arms, and shoulders with coconut oil, and Koa fed him roast pig and vegetables. Afterwards the priests followed Cook back to his boat with adoring courtesy.

Idol from the Sandwich Islands, known now as Hawaii

James Cook had traveled around the world. His voyages into the Pacific Ocean had won him fame and honor as the greatest explorer of his age. But he had never experienced such remarkable attention as these natives showed him.

In truth, the Hawaiians believed Cook was Rono, their god of peace and happiness. According to legend, Rono had sailed away from Hawaii long ago, promising to return one day on a ship carrying a forest of small trees. Now, for the second time in less than a year, the sudden sight of two ships whose masts looked like trees left Hawaiians certain that Rono had returned.

The natives stared in astonishment at the British sailors anchored in their bay. These strange visitors carried fire burning in their mouths (pipes) and drew out anything they needed from holes in their loose skins (jacket pockets). Some men had pointy heads (officers' three-cornered hats), and others could remove the tops of their heads (wigs). Surely the leader of such amazing creatures must be the wonderful god Rono.

For two weeks the Hawaiians gladly helped the strangers in any way they could. After giving away much of their food, however, they began to wonder when the ships would leave. The British never seemed to tire of eating, and Lieutenant James King noticed how the natives began "stroking the sides and patting the bellies of the sailors . . . telling them partly by signs and partly by words that it was time for them to go." At last, repairs on the *Resolution* and the *Discovery* were finished, and on February 4, 1779, Captain Cook ordered sails hoisted. As the ships left Kealakekua Bay, all of the crew members still marveled at the generous treatment they had received.

The little British fleet sailed north directly into a tropical storm. On the night of February 7, roaring waves crashed over the wooden decks and howling winds whipped through the sails. Suddenly the foremast of the *Resolution* cracked and sprang out of place. Captain Cook realized that the ship needed immediate repairs before more serious damage occurred. Fatefully he turned back toward Kealakekua Bay.

On February 11, the *Resolution* and the *Discovery* glided again over the smooth water that led into the bay. But the expectant smiles vanished from the faces of the British sailors as they blinked and gazed around. No celebrating Hawaiians greeted them this time. The bay and its beaches stood strangely deserted and silent. Having mapped the vast Pacific Ocean from the Arctic to Antarctica, Captain Cook was soon to meet his tragic death in Kealakekua Bay.

Kealakekua Bay

Chapter 2
Born for the Sea

Smoke curled from the chimney of a humble, two-room clay cottage in the village of Marton-in-Cleveland on October 27, 1728. The loud cries of a baby announced the birth of James Cook, Jr., the second child of James Cook and Grace Pace Cook. Soon afterwards, the growing family carted their belongings to a larger cottage in the same neighborhood. James Cook, Sr. was a hardy Scotsman who worked as a hired farm laborer in the Yorkshire section of England. While his mother sewed and cooked, little James romped across the clay floor playing with his older brother, John, and the five other boys and girls born into the family.

While still a youngster, James often helped his mother with household chores. He fetched pails of water and carried bundles of firewood. Sometimes he followed his father to work at farms in the nearby village of Ayton. Together father and son herded sheep, cleaned horse stalls, and piled stone along the edges of cleared fields.

At one farm called Marton Grange, young James watered horses and ran errands. The farmer's wife, Mrs. Walker, admired James's cheerful spirit. Often she invited him into the house, where she showed him books and taught him the alphabet. In 1736, James's father moved his family to Ayton. Through hard work, he had risen to the job of manager on Thomas Skottowe's Airyholme Farm.

The Cooks wished something better than the farming life for their growing son James. The eight-year-old seemed bright and promising, and Mr. Skottowe generously agreed to pay for James's schooling. At the Postgate School in Ayton, James joined other local children at wooden desks and learned reading, writing, and arithmetic. After school, he raced through the village streets with his friends, hiked the countryside in search of birds' nests, and helped his father with Airyholme farm work.

James proved a good student and showed skill with numbers. Sometime around 1740, Mr. Cook found his son an opportunity as a shopkeeper's apprentice. Several miles east of Ayton, the village of Staithes stood on the English coast overlooking the North Sea. In William Sanderson's general store, young James swept the floors and dusted shelves. He wrapped cheese, crackers, and other grocery items for customers. Upon the counter he measured and cut ribbons and cloth, and at the till he carefully counted out change. Often, though, the teenager's mind wandered to the world beyond the shop's doors.

Along the Staithes docks, fishermen sang while they repaired their nets. Skilled shipwrights hammered and chiseled at wooden hulls and tall, straight masts. Seagulls soared over the rocky shoreline, while in the distance showed the white squares of merchant ships' sails as they passed up and down the coast. The glory of the sea filled young James Cook with excitement. He used every spare moment to ramble along the waterfront and deeply breathe the smell of salt and tar. He listened keenly when the local sailors talked about their work, and gladly he rowed about the harbor whenever they invited him to join them.

Life in a general store seemed dull indeed compared with a life at sea. For months James pleaded with his employer for a chance to become an apprentice sailor instead of a grocer's apprentice. At last, in 1746, Mr. Sanderson took the seventeen-year-old to the neighboring town of Whitby. There John Walker agreed to take Cook into service.

Walker and his brother Henry owned several sturdy, broad-bottomed ships of a style called Whitby Cats. The Walkers regularly shipped coal from the mining town of Newcastle down the coast and up the Thames River to London. Eagerly Cook shipped aboard the 341-ton (304-metric-ton) coalship *Freelove* as an apprentice seaman.

For three years James Cook learned the sailing craft. The experienced crewmen taught him how to tie sailors' knots and how to climb into the rigging to trim the sails. Ship's officers showed him how to read the points of a compass and how to measure latitude by using an instrument called a quadrant. At night Cook studied the constellations in the starry sky. By day, he learned every mile of the crooked English coastline. During stormy winter months, the Walkers kept their ships moored at Whitby. Cook spent that time at John Walker's house carefully examining sailing charts and books on navigation by flickering candlelight.

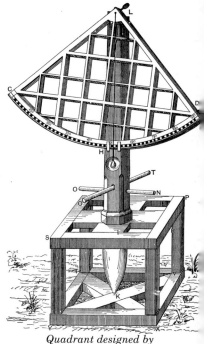

Quadrant designed by astronomer Tycho Brahe

15

In time, young James earned the rank of able seaman. Aboard such Walker ships as the *Three Brothers* and the *Friendship*, he proved his skills by safely steering along the dangerous coast. At the age of twenty-four, the Walkers rewarded Cook by promoting him to the rank of ship's mate.

The hardships of the sailing life failed to dampen the spirits of James Cook. As second-in-command, the tall, strong young ship's mate saw his Whitby Cats through many hazardous situations. During one raging coastal storm, his vessel rolled and lurched through foaming waves. At the last moment, Cook steered clear of another coalship too damaged to save itself from sinking.

Royal Navy ships assembled at Spithead, England

It soon became obvious to the Walker brothers that James Cook was no common sailor. In 1755, they offered him command of the *Friendship*. As the respected captain of a coalship, Cook's future would be assured. But he wanted something more, and his ambition drove him to make an important decision. At the age of twenty-seven, he abandoned the Whitby coal trade. Instead, he volunteered to join Great Britain's Royal Navy as an able seaman. The Seven Years' War, called the French and Indian War in America, was on the verge of erupting in Europe. Great Britain's Royal Navy needed every experienced seaman it could get for its fight against France. Having determined to try his fortune in the navy, Cook signed up in the town of Wapping on June 17, 1755.

Cook's orders carried him south to the English seaport of Portsmouth. There he climbed aboard the great sixty-gun warship *Eagle*. Although it was four times the size of the *Friendship*, Cook refused to let the *Eagle* overwhelm him. With quiet skill, he assisted in the refitting of the ship. Side by side with his fellow seamen, he sanded the decks, caulked and tarred the hull, replaced worn sails, and straightened knotted rigging. In just five short weeks, Cook proved himself such an able sailor that he was promoted to master's mate. The master was the ship's chief navigator, and as master's mate Cook would be his assistant.

Through the summer months, the *Eagle* cruised off the coast of Ireland. In the fall a new captain, Hugh Palliser, stepped aboard the warship. He promoted Cook to the important position of boatswain, the sailor chiefly responsible for the ship's ropes, sails, cables, anchors, flags, and boats. Through the next months, the *Eagle* patrolled along the western coast of France.

On May 25, 1756, cannon roared as the *Eagle* and another British ship, the *Medway*, attacked the fifty-gun French merchant ship *Duc d'Aquitaine*. "The Fire was very brisk on both sides for near an hour," exclaimed Captain Palliser. Dozens of British sailors fell dead or wounded as cannonballs and grapeshot smashed through the *Eagle*'s hull and tore across the deck. Cook survived, though, and as the smoke cleared he cheered the surrender of the French ship.

The damaged *Eagle* sailed to Plymouth on the southern coast of England for repairs. While there, Captain Palliser decided Cook had earned the right to be promoted to ship's master. As the *Eagle*'s chief navigator, Cook worked closely with Captain Palliser, and in time the two became firm friends.

In October 1757, the British Admiralty transferred twenty-nine-year-old Master Cook to the sixty-four-gun *Pembroke* commanded by Captain John Simcoe. With the help of Captain Simcoe and military engineer Samuel Holland, Cook continued his study of mathematics, astronomy, and surveying techniques.

In the spring of 1758, the *Pembroke* joined a great British fleet of troopships assembling at Halifax, Nova Scotia, on the northeastern tip of North America. While the British possessed thirteen colonies along the North American coast, the French controlled much of Canada, then known as New France, to the north. Now the British planned to attack New France's colonial capital of Quebec on the St. Lawrence River.

The French fortress of Louisbourg on the eastern tip of Nova Scotia presented the first challenge to the British. It guarded the mouth of the St. Lawrence River. Over choppy waters, boats carried regiments of soldiers ashore at Louisbourg. From the deck of the

The port of Halifax, Nova Scotia

Pembroke, Cook watched these British troops day after day as they fought their way closer to the fortress. On July 26, 1758, cannon boomed in celebration aboard the *Pembroke* as the British flag waved from Louisbourg signaling the French surrender. The St. Lawrence River, the route to Quebec, now lay open to the British.

The British fleet easily sailed up the St. Lawrence River in the autumn of 1758. Just before reaching Quebec, however, the ships stopped. The stretch of river that lay ahead was narrow and choked with dangerous sandbars and rocky reefs. The British captains needed detailed knowledge of the river before making their attack. Now Admiral Sir Charles Saunders chose Cook and a few other ship's masters to chart the river and find a safe channel for the fleet to follow.

The death of General Wolfe

Bravely Cook and his assistants took up their work. The forts of Quebec stood upon a high bluff overlooking the river. Within range of French cannon, Cook and his men rowed along the shoreline, usually at night, carefully drawing maps and measuring the water's depth. The dangerous and difficult duty took many months, through winter snowstorms and icy rains. On one occasion the French sent some of their Indian allies to attack the British surveyors. With piercing war cries, the Indians sprang from the shoreline. Cook escaped capture by leaping from the bow of his boat just as several warriors climbed aboard.

At last Cook finished his detailed charts of the river. On June 25, 1759, the British fleet of 22 warships and 119 troopships successfully sailed through the St. Lawrence narrows. Once past the river fortresses, General James Wolfe landed nine thousand British Redcoats and began his siege of Quebec. Although Wolfe died during the bloody fight, Quebec finally surrendered on September 18.

James Cook could be proud of the vital role he played in this tremendous British victory. His fine river charts soon gained the attention of Lord Alexander Colville, new admiral of the British fleet. Colville chose Master Cook to perform navigating duties aboard his flagship, the *Northumberland*. During 1760 and 1761, the *Northumberland* slowly sailed from Quebec back to the Atlantic Ocean. Carefully Cook surveyed and drew charts of the entire length of the St. Lawrence River.

Lord Colville thanked Cook for his service by awarding him the sum of fifty pounds on January 19, 1761, "in consideration of his . . . industry in making himself master of the pilotage of the river St.

Lawrence." Sending the charts on to London, Colville informed the Lords of the British Admiralty "that from my experience of Mr. Cook's genius and capacity I think him well qualified for . . . greater undertakings of the same kind."

At the age of thirty-three, James Cook, the Yorkshire farm boy, had earned a reputation as perhaps the best surveyor and navigator in the entire Royal Navy.

Full-length engraving of Captain James Cook, mariner and explorer

Chapter 3
"Very Expert in His Business"

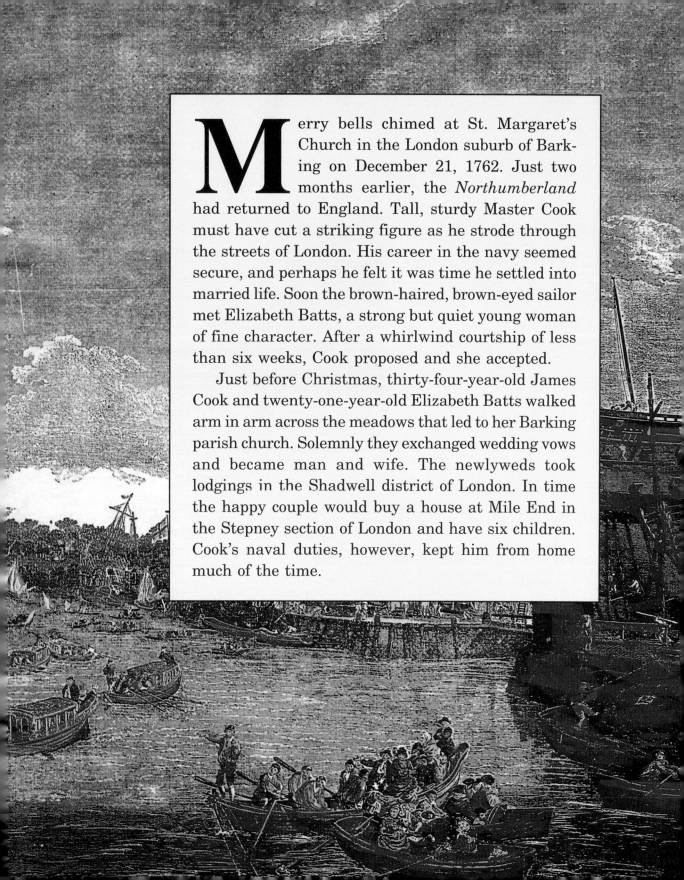

Merry bells chimed at St. Margaret's Church in the London suburb of Barking on December 21, 1762. Just two months earlier, the *Northumberland* had returned to England. Tall, sturdy Master Cook must have cut a striking figure as he strode through the streets of London. His career in the navy seemed secure, and perhaps he felt it was time he settled into married life. Soon the brown-haired, brown-eyed sailor met Elizabeth Batts, a strong but quiet young woman of fine character. After a whirlwind courtship of less than six weeks, Cook proposed and she accepted.

Just before Christmas, thirty-four-year-old James Cook and twenty-one-year-old Elizabeth Batts walked arm in arm across the meadows that led to her Barking parish church. Solemnly they exchanged wedding vows and became man and wife. The newlyweds took lodgings in the Shadwell district of London. In time the happy couple would buy a house at Mile End in the Stepney section of London and have six children. Cook's naval duties, however, kept him from home much of the time.

King George III

The Treaty of Paris, signed in February 1763, ended the Seven Years' War with a British victory. King George III wished careful surveys made of the vast Canadian territories he now controlled. The Lords of the Admiralty assigned Cook the task of mapping the unknown coast of the Canadian island of Newfoundland. As a surveyor Cook would earn ten shillings a day, better pay than a navy lieutenant earned.

In May 1763, Cook sailed aboard the *Antelope* across the Atlantic Ocean. At Newfoundland he and his assistants carried ashore the theodolite, telescopic quadrant, and other surveying equipment needed for their work. Captain Thomas Graves, military governor of Newfoundland, ordered the team to "make Charts of all the said Coasts, with Drafts of the Harbors, noting the Depths of Water and Conveniences for fishing, and whatever Observations may Occur worthy of our knowledge."

Carefully Cook began the difficult task of surveying the 6,000 miles (9,656 kilometers) of jagged Newfoundland coastline. Not a single rocky cove or river inlet escaped his notice. Mile after mile, he marked every coastal curve and recorded the depth of the seaside waters. During the sticky days of summer, clouds of flies and mosquitoes pestered him. In the winter he returned to England to draw detailed maps of the coast.

Sailing back to Newfoundland in the spring of 1764, Cook happily discovered that his friend Sir Hugh Palliser had been named new military governor of the island. Greatly impressed with Cook's work, Palliser asked him to extend his survey north and map the 2,000-mile (3,219-kilometer) coastline of Labrador as well. He gave Cook command of the 70-ton (62.5-

metric-ton) schooner HMS *Grenville*. The sails of the *Grenville* flapped in the breeze as Cook dutifully pushed north along the Newfoundland coast. Day after day, leadsmen rowed boats ahead and dropped lines to sound the depth of the water. Stepping ashore, Cook set up his instruments and made mathematical calculations of heights and distances.

On August 6, 1764, a freak gunpowder accident nearly ended his career as a surveyor. That day, Ship's Mate William Parker penned in the *Grenville* logbook: "2 pm. Came on board the Cutter with the Master [Cook] who unfortunately had a Large Powder Horn blown up and Burst in his hand which shatter'd it in a Terrible manner." The explosion broke bones and deeply gashed Cook's right hand between his thumb and forefinger. A surgeon bandaged the awful wound and, though in constant pain, Cook was back at work a month later.

The difficult job of surveying both Newfoundland and Labrador kept Cook busy from 1763 until 1767. He spent every winter in England drawing maps with quill pens and colored inks. These finished charts were so perfect that commercial fishermen and naval officers used them without change for the next one hundred years. The Lords of the Admiralty now spoke of Cook as the navy's finest surveyor. He also became known to the scientists of the Royal Society of London. In August 1766, Cook had observed a total eclipse of the sun while in Canada. He sent his scientific notes of the event to the Royal Society, whose grateful members soon announced Cook "a good mathematician and very expert in his business." Both the Royal Navy and the Royal Society began to suspect that James Cook was just the man they were looking for.

For centuries, the Pacific Ocean had remained a tempting mystery to Europeans. In 1488, Portuguese sailor Bartolomeu Dias had first discovered a route toward the Pacific by sailing around Africa's Cape of Good Hope. In 1513, Spanish explorer Vasco Núñez de Balboa crossed the Isthmus of Panama and was the first European to gaze upon its waters from the east. Ferdinand Magellan crossed the Pacific after passing through narrow straits at the tip of South America in 1521. In 1578, English adventurer Sir Francis Drake successfully rounded South America's Cape Horn. Through the next two hundred years,

The straits of Magellan at the tip of South America

other Europeans followed these pioneering paths into the Pacific Ocean.

Spanish, Dutch, French, and English explorers all ventured into the mighty Pacific in search of fame and fortune. Curious sailors briefly touched upon the northern and western coasts of Australia. Dutchman Abel Tasman sighted Van Diemen's Land (Tasmania) and New Zealand in 1642. European ships skirted along the coasts of New Guinea and Pacific islands such as Tahiti, the Solomons, and the New Hebrides. Every voyage had added to the knowledge of the Pacific. But the ocean measured 10,000 miles (16,093 kilometers) from Asia to America and 9,000 miles (14,484 kilometers) from the Arctic to Antarctica. Its waters covered an area greater than all the land on earth. Even by the 1760s, most of the Pacific remained unknown.

Ancient geographers believed that a huge, undiscovered "Southern Continent" gave balance to the lands of the earth's Northern Hemisphere. Through the centuries, European scholars imagined this continent covered the whole southern surface of the earth and possessed rich civilizations. Surely the European nation that discovered the Southern Continent would gain immense power and wealth.

On May 19, 1768, Captain Samuel Wallis returned to England from a round-the-world voyage. While crossing the Pacific, he excitedly reported, he and his men believed they had sighted mountains rising in the distance to the south. "We supposed," he later declared, that "we saw the long wished for Southern Continent, which has never before been seen by Europeans." Eagerly King George III urged the Lords of the British Admiralty to plan another Pacific voyage.

The Royal Society took keen interest in this expedition. They wished to send an astronomer to the South Pacific to observe the Transit of Venus—the passage of Venus between the earth and sun, predicted for 1769. Sir Alexander Dalrymple of the Royal Society insisted he was just the man to lead the entire voyage. As a scholarly geographer, Dalrymple had long promoted the theory of the Southern Continent. He thought he knew more about it than anyone alive. As an amateur astronomer, he also claimed he could observe the Transit of Venus and record that important event for the Royal Society.

A committee of the Navy Board carefully discussed the situation. From the committee's point of view, this Pacific voyage required the skills of an expert navigator and surveyor. Forty-year-old James Cook had proven himself well in these areas. In the end, the committee decided that Cook, rather than Dalrymple, was the ideal person to lead the voyage. On May 25, 1768, he was promoted to the rank of lieutenant and was given command of the expedition.

In a matter of days, Lieutenant Cook walked the docks of Deptford Navy Yard on the Thames River. Happily he looked upon the ship assigned to carry him on his Pacific journey. By strange luck, it was a kind of ship with which Cook was totally familiar. In March, the Navy Board had suggested that a "cat-built vessel" be purchased "which in their kind are roomy and will afford the advantage of stowing and carrying a large quantity of provision so necessary on such voyages." Navy purchasing officers soon chose a Whitby coalship named the *Earl of Pembroke*.

The 368-ton (334-metric-ton) vessel measured 106 feet (32 meters) in length. Built for hard use rather

Cook's ship HMS Endeavour

than graceful beauty, the ship possessed a squared stern and a broad bow. Measuring 29 feet (9 meters) in width, the hull provided ample storage space. The draught of the ship, meaning the depth of its hull under water, was only 11 feet (3.3 meters). It could safely sail close to uncharted shores. Lightly rigged and easy to handle, the ship was small enough to be beached and repaired if damaged. After walking its deck, Cook declared, "In such a vessel an able sea officer will be more venturesome and better enabled to fulfill his instructions than he possibly can in one of any other sort or size." The Royal Navy renamed the ship HMS *Endeavour*.

For months, workers in the Deptford yard prepared the sturdy little ship for its voyage. Ship's carpenters hammered a second skin of planking to the hull and studded it with flat-headed nails. This was for protection against dreaded seaworms that lived by boring into wood. In the large cargo hold, they built a new deck where the common sailors could hang their net hammocks. Some workers caulked the seams of the deck planking, while others refitted masts and spars. Sailmakers cut and sewed great squares of canvas. Armorers hauled aboard brass cannons, and ship's chandlers carried spare ropes, anchors, and other equipment below deck. Up the gangway, laborers rolled great casks and barrels filled with water, rum, biscuits, cheese, salted meat, and other preserved foods.

On this voyage, Cook decided to conduct an experiment. For centuries, sailors on long voyages had suffered from a disease called scurvy. It caused joints and gums to swell and teeth to fall out. In the end, victims often died. Seagoing sailors often lived on salted meat, oatmeal, wormy biscuits, and a little cheese or butter, all washed down with beer or rum. Some scientists believed it was this poor diet that caused scurvy.

Cook considered it very important to have fruit and green vegetables aboard his ship. Besides the usual shipboard foods, he loaded barrels of sauerkraut (pickled cabbage), malt, and dried soups. Sailors carried aboard cases of bottled orange and lemon juice and vinegar. Cook was sure that, by feeding his men a balanced diet, he could prevent sickness and death from scurvy.

The Royal Navy assigned eighty-four sailors to join Cook aboard the *Endeavour*: officers, mates, marines, and able-bodied crewmen. Upset that Cook had received the command, Sir Alexander Dalrymple bitterly refused to take further part in the expedition. The Royal Society assigned his place to Charles Green, assistant to the royal astronomer, and trusted that with Cook's help the Transit of Venus would be recorded properly.

Another member of the Royal Society also eagerly joined the voyage. Rich and well-educated, twenty-five-year-old Joseph Banks excitedly grabbed at this opportunity to explore the world and win fame as a natural scientist.

At his own expense, Banks brought with him the noted naturalist Dr. Daniel Solander and Hermann Sporing as assistant naturalist. He brought two artists named Alexander Buchan and Sydney Parkinson to make drawings of all the sea life, plant life, and animal life they would see.

Banks also brought four personal servants, who carried aboard cases of jars for specimens and presses for plants; easels, brushes, and paints for drawing; inks, pens, and notebooks for writing; nets for catching insects; and hooks and lines for fishing. It was enough gear to turn the *Endeavour* into a floating scientific laboratory.

In high spirits, Banks crowded his scientific party aboard and even brought along two pet greyhounds. Perhaps Cook scratched his head and grimly wondered where everything would fit. Nevertheless, workers at Plymouth Harbor finally tightened the last bolt and crammed the last chest of gear below deck. On August 25, 1768, Captain Cook looked on as the boatswain barked orders to the crew. Hoisted sails puffed large as the *Endeavour* glided out of port and started upon its great adventure.

Chapter 4
The Endeavour

Salt water sprayed over the bow as the ship *Endeavour* rolled forward through the ocean waves. Masts and planking creaked with a regular rhythm. Agile sailors scampered high aloft among the rigging. As they trimmed the sails, they felt cool breezes and gusts of wind blow across their cheeks.

Though most of the *Endeavour*'s sailors were young, still they were ocean veterans. Five of the men had sailed with Cook aboard the *Grenville*. Five others had journeyed around the world aboard Captain Wallis's ship the *Dolphin*. Many of these sailors no longer felt at home on land. The comforts and excitement of the sailing life constantly drew them back to the sea. These seamen knew their duties, and under Captain Cook's commanding eye they performed them well.

During its first weeks, the *Endeavour* sailed south to the Madeira Islands off the coast of North Africa. In the Madeiras the ship took on casks of the fine local wines, fresh water, fruit, and sacks of onions. On September 18, 1768, the *Endeavour* steered southward, where it picked up the trade winds that would carry it west to South America.

Beneath the bright blue sky the ship pitched along. Happy sailors smoked pipes and tossed fishing lines from the sides of the ship. Their thoughtful captain had separated the crew into three watches instead of the normal two. This allowed the men more time for sleeping and relaxing and kept them in good spirits.

Joseph Banks lay seasick in his cabin during the first days of the voyage. In time, though, Banks grew used to the rolling waves and enjoyed the open sea. The ocean's wildlife delighted him and his scientific team. Porpoises sometimes playfully swam beside the ship. Seabirds often whirled above the sails. Casting nets, Banks and his men caught interesting fish. On calm days they rowed the ship's boats about, observing plankton, jellyfish, and other sea life.

On November 13, the *Endeavour* finished its Atlantic crossing. The little ship cruised into the coastal harbor of Rio de Janeiro, Brazil. Captain Cook expected a friendly welcome from Great Britain's Portuguese allies in Rio de Janeiro. Instead, Antonio Rolim de Moura, the Portuguese viceroy of Brazil, greeted the ship with deep suspicion. The *Endeavour* looked like no Royal Navy ship he had ever seen before. He guessed Cook and his crew were smugglers or perhaps even spies. Under Portuguese guard, the viceroy allowed a boat to land and buy food and gather water. While Cook purchased meat, vegetables, and fruit, most of his crew remained on board caulking leaks and repairing rigging. At last on December 7, the *Endeavour* sailed from the troublesome harbor.

Cook was willing to try anything to save the lives of his men. He had purchased onions in the Madeiras and fresh fruit and vegetables in Rio de Janeiro in hopes of giving the *Endeavour*'s crew a varied and

healthful diet. Every day he ordered his sailors to eat the strange foods he had stocked, though they often resisted. Cook used a trick to start them eating sauerkraut. He announced that it was only being served to the officers. He knew that when sailors "see their Superiors set a value upon it, it becomes the finest stuff in the world." Sure enough, within a week, all the common sailors demanded that they be allowed to eat sauerkraut, too.

Cook also believed that cleanliness aboard the *Endeavour* would help keep the men healthy and free of scurvy. Under his orders, the men washed regularly with salt water. In the galley, the ship's cook scrubbed pots, pans, and utensils. From time to time the sailors dragged their bedding onto deck for airing. Clothes were washed in soapy tubs, and pots of smoking coals were set below deck to rid the ship of rats and lice.

As the *Endeavour* sailed southward, Captain Cook insisted that his crew dress warmly and stay dry. Overcoats and woolen trousers helped to fight the chilly weather in those lower latitudes. By the middle of January 1769, the ship reached Tierra del Fuego, the island at the southern tip of South America. The island's rocky coast and ice-capped mountains hardly seemed inviting. But on January 16 Cook landed his boats in order to gather wood and water at a place called the Bay of Success.

Joseph Banks, his scientific assistants, his servants, and a few sailors wandered inland to collect plants and other natural specimens. The men climbed high into the hills overlooking the bay. Before they could return, however, darkness fell and a biting snowstorm began. For hours Banks forced the weary men to keep tramping along. He understood the danger of stopping to rest in this freezing weather. Sadly, two of his servants lay down, and they died of the cold during the night. Banks and the others survived with difficulty. In the night they huddled around a small fire of sticks, and in the morning they stumbled back to the warmth of the *Endeavour*.

Weighing anchor, the voyagers pressed onward. At the end of January, the *Endeavour* rounded Cape Horn in unusually calm weather. Now, with the Atlantic Ocean at his back, Captain Cook gazed for the first time at the Pacific. During his world cruise, Captain Wallis had rediscovered the islands of Tahiti, first discovered by the Portuguese sailor Pedro de Queiros in 1606. Wallis had described them as a lovely haven in the middle of the South Pacific. As a result, Tahiti had been chosen as the place from which to observe the Transit of Venus.

Cape Froward and Mount Victoria, Chile, at South America's tip

Through February and March the *Endeavour* bounded in a northwesterly direction over the green South Pacific waves. The wind grew softer and the air turned warmer. The crewmen shucked off their heavy clothes and eagerly listened to delightful tales of Tahiti as told by the five veterans who had been there. On April 4, a lookout in the forward rigging shouted. The *Endeavour* had chanced upon its first Pacific island. Cook named the sandy little reef Lagoon Island (present-day Vahitahi). The ship continued westward past other islands of the Tahiti chain. Cook decided to call the group the Society Islands, in honor of the Royal Society.

Pineapple of Tahiti

At last, on April 11, the high green mountains of the island of Tahiti rose on the horizon. On April 13 the *Endeavour* coasted into the curving bay Captain Wallis had visited. The waters of Matavai Bay splashed about the hull as the *Endeavour* dropped its anchor.

From the beach, natives paddled out in finely carved canoes. *"Taio! Taio!"* they shouted, meaning "Friend! Friend!" Bringing gifts of coconuts and fruit, they cheerfully welcomed the foreigners. According to Captain Wallis, the Tahitians yearned for metal of any kind. Any favor could be purchased with a common iron nail. The *Endeavour*, therefore, came prepared with kegs full of nails and spikes for trading.

During the next days the sailors pitched tents and made camp ashore. Joseph Banks conducted a general marketplace for the expedition, exchanging nails for hogs, fruit, and vegetables. His scientific party

Palm tree growing out over the water on Tahiti's coast

spread across the island collecting samples of plants, flowers, and insects. At the same time, Captain Cook and astronomer Charles Green found an excellent spot where they would watch the Transit of Venus when the day arrived. They called it Venus Point, and Cook had his men cut trees and build a little fort there.

Throughout each day, the Tahitians and their British visitors happily mingled together. To most of the crew, Tahiti seemed like heaven. Fragrant breezes blew through swaying palm leaves. Laughing Tahitian women wore flowers in their hair and danced. The natives were clean, friendly, and generous. One Tahitian habit, though, greatly annoyed Captain Cook. In his journal he soon complained, "They are thieves to a Man and would steal but everything that came in their way . . . with such [skill] as would shame the most noted pickpocket in Europe."

Flowers growing in Tahiti's rich volcanic soil

During their first day ashore, a native picked the pocket of Dr. Solander and carried off his spyglass. Dr. Monkhouse, the ship's surgeon, later slapped his pockets and discovered his snuffbox stolen. During a night ashore, Cook carefully tucked his stockings under his pillow for safekeeping. In the morning they were gone. One bold theft sadly ended in death. A native snatched a musket from the hands of a British sentry. As the thief ran away, another guard fired and shot the Tahitian down.

A farmyard scene in Tahiti after Europeans had introduced farm animals to the island

Another serious incident occurred when Cook and Charles Green prepared to set up their quadrant on Venus Point. The valuable instrument was gone. "It had never been taken out of the Packing case," Cook later exclaimed, "and the whole was pretty heavy, so that it was a matter of astonishment to us all how it could be taken away." Angrily Joseph Banks chased into the jungle after the thief. He and Charles Green managed to find the quadrant in pieces and they brought it back.

On June 3, 1769, all was ready on Venus Point. Cook and Green stared through their telescopes and recorded distances with the quadrant as the planet Venus eclipsed the sun. Throughout the world on that day, other astronomers also watched the historic event. They hoped that, by comparing mathematical data, they could calculate the distance of the earth from the sun and measure the size of the solar system. Unfortunately, they later realized that a cloud around the planet Venus made this particular study valueless no matter how carefully made.

In any event, Cook had faithfully carried out the first part of his duty in the South Pacific. Having observed the Transit of Venus, he tore open the sealed envelope that contained his secret instructions for the next part of the voyage.

"You are to proceed to the southward in order to make discovery of the Continent," the British Admiralty document read. The *Endeavour* was to sail south of Tahiti in search of the Southern Continent. Sir Alexander Dalrymple had insisted that New Zealand was a peninsula of the mysterious continent. If possible, Cook was to determine if that theory were true or not.

Tears filled the eyes of some sailors as the *Endeavour* raised anchor at last on July 13. They had grown to love Tahiti, and some men would have deserted ship if they could. Along the beach of Matavai Bay, the Tahitians sadly watched their British friends hoist sails. "For some time before we left this Island," Cook later wrote, "several of the natives were daily offering themselves to go away with us, and as it was thought that they must be of use to us in our future discoveries, we resolved to bring away one whose name is Tupia, a Chief and a Priest."

With Tupia aboard, the *Endeavour* sailed away and explored among a few of the other Tahitian islands before turning southward. During the next six weeks, the ship pounded ahead through uncharted waters. At the 40-degree-south latitude, Cook turned the *Endeavour* to the west. According to Abel Tasman's reports of his 1642 exploration, New Zealand would be found along the 40-degree latitude. Therefore Cook struggled along that course.

On October 6, 1769, Joseph Banks excitedly penned in his journal, "At 1/2 Past One a Small Boy who was at the masthead call'd out Land!"

Cook ordered that the *Endeavour* steer toward the distant outline. The next day the ship reached the coast of New Zealand. Cook named the point of land Young Nick's Head, after Nicholas Young, the ship's boy who first sighted it.

Cook rowed ashore with a landing party and soon encountered natives of the group called the Maori. Remarkably, when Tupia spoke, these natives understood his Polynesian language. Unlike the smiling Tahitians, however, the Maoris displayed no friendliness. Regarding all strangers as enemies, they waved

Dutch explorer Abel Tasman

Maori chief of New Zealand

spears and clubs so fiercely that Cook ordered musket volleys fired over their heads. Finally the sailors were forced to shoot and kill one ferocious native "just as he was going to dart his spear at the boat," recounted Cook.

The next day while rowing near shore, Cook and a boatload of sailors encountered other natives paddling in canoes. These Maoris snatched up their weapons and again Cook felt forced to open fire. "Two or three were kill'd, and one wounded, and three jumped over board," he sadly remembered of the fight.

Cook named this spot Poverty Bay because he got no fresh water, wood, or welcome there. From Poverty Bay, the *Endeavour* sailed south for some time without finding a good harbor. Cook steered the ship back toward the north. On December 14 the *Endeavour* rounded the northernmost tip of New Zealand, which Cook named North Cape. Other capes, bays, and harbors presented themselves as the ship next scudded southward along the western coast.

When a 30-mile (48-kilometer) gap opened in the coastline, the *Endeavour* sailed forward. Cook named the place Queen Charlotte's Sound, and in the calm waters of a sheltered cove, he ordered the anchor dropped. During the second half of January 1770, crewmen rowed ashore and sawed timber for new mast pieces and filled barrels with water from gurgling streams.

On the morning of January 26, Cook, Banks, and Dr. Solander climbed a high hill and made a startling discovery. Gazing eastward, they realized that Queen Charlotte's Sound opened into a strait that separated two bodies of land. Instantly Cook saw that at least the northern part of New Zealand was an island. In a formal flag-raising ceremony five days later, Cook claimed Queen Charlotte's Sound for Great Britain. The next week, the *Endeavour* entered the narrow waters of what came to be called Cook Strait. Many of the ship's officers still believed the southern part of New Zealand was attached to the Southern Continent. Cook now sailed south to explore the southern New Zealand coast.

Gusting winds and rainstorms challenged Cook's sailing skills. The deadly danger of submerged rocks and underwater reefs threatened the *Endeavour*

New Zealand's Cook Strait

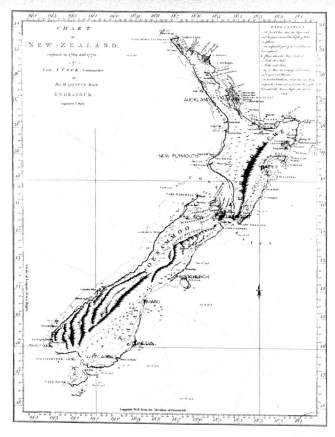

Map of New Zealand based on Cook's own chart, showing the route Cook traveled around the islands

whenever it ventured close to shore. But Cook took his ship where no European had ever dared. "No country upon earth can appear with a more rugged and barren aspect than this doth from the sea," declared Cook. By the middle of March, however, he had sailed around New Zealand's southern tip and had started up the western coast. By March 24, the *Endeavour* once more had reached Queen Charlotte's Sound. The rough sea journey had proven without a doubt that New Zealand consisted of two islands without connection to the fabled Southern Continent.

The *Endeavour* gently rocked as Captain Cook sat in his cabin and dipped his quill pen in ink. "As to a southern continent," he now jotted in his journal, "I do not believe any such thing exists unless in a high latitude [near the South Pole]."

Chapter 5
"The Ship Struck and
Stuck Fast"

Crewmen and passengers all yearned for home. Worn sails, frayed ropes, and dribbling leaks in the hull showed the hard service already performed by the *Endeavour*. After nineteen months of traveling, Captain Cook agreed it was time to return to England. Free to choose his own homeward route, he decided to sail west. He hoped to investigate the uncharted eastern coast of Australia and afterwards stop at the Dutch trading colony of Batavia in Java before starting the long journey home.

On April 1, 1770, the coast of New Zealand disappeared behind the *Endeavour*. For seventeen days, the little ship plowed westward through the foaming ocean. Cook never knew what he might discover in this unknown region of the world. The crude maps drawn in 1642 by the Dutch explorer Abel Tasman made even the coast of Australia an uncertain target. At dawn on April 19, Lieutenant Zachary Hicks spied a low stretch of coastline on the western horizon. Cook called this first Australian landfall Point Hicks in honor of his sharp-eyed young officer, and he named the entire region New South Wales.

Aborigine bark painting

From there, Cook followed Australia's coastline northward. "At daylight in the morning," he wrote on April 28, "we discovered a Bay which appeared to be tolerably well sheltered from all winds." The anchor splashed as the *Endeavour* came to rest in this bay.

Dark-skinned, naked natives stood on the beach as a ship's boat rowed through the water. Two natives raised spears when Cook and his shore party cautiously neared. Tupia tried speaking to these Australian natives, called aborigines, but they did not understand the Polynesian language. When Cook ordered warning shots fired, the two startled aborigines hurled their spears and ran away.

In the following days, Cook and his sailors made other efforts to communicate, but the aborigines showed little interest in their strange visitors. They simply wished to be left alone. "We could know but very little of their customs," admitted Cook, "as we never were able to form any connections with them."

During their stay in this bay, hungry sailors fished while Banks and Dr. Solander eagerly tramped through the inland woods. Colorful cockatoos and parrots flew among the branches of tall gum trees. In their jars and little wooden boxes, the scientists collected a wealth of strange leaves and flowers. The two men spoke so excitedly of the region's botany, or plant life, that Cook called the harbor Botany Bay.

On May 7, the *Endeavour* sailed onward. As he looked west, Cook noted the shape of hundreds of miles of previously uncharted coastline. He could not sail too close to this unknown shore. Hidden rocks and shoals could smash his little ship in an instant. When he gazed to the east, however, Cook soon realized that danger lay in that direction, too.

The Great Barrier Reef stood 150 miles (241 kilometers) off shore at its starting point off Australia's southern coast. But every mile that the *Endeavour* passed to the north, the reef curved closer to the land. With the mainland on one side and the reef on the other, Cook had sailed into a very dangerous funnel. Stretching 1,200 miles (1,931 kilometers), the Great Barrier Reef is the largest reef in the world. Amazingly, reefs are made of the skeletons of tiny sea animals called coral polyps. Massed together in rock-hard formations, the coral rises in jagged ridges from the ocean floor.

By the first days of June, Cook knew he had entered a deadly zone of reefs. Carefully he zigzagged his ship north through the constant maze of coral hazards that lay just beneath the ocean's surface. At every moment, lookouts stared at the waves ahead searching for signs of coral. A leadsman always stood at the bow, throwing a weighted line overboard to measure the depth of the water.

All day on June 11, the *Endeavour* picked its way through hills and valleys of underwater reefs. By evening it seemed the ship had reached an area of deep water. A bright moon shone upon the smooth, calm sea as the *Endeavour* slowly glided ahead. Wearily, Captain Cook lay down in his cabin to take a rest.

At 11:00, the leadsman tossed his line into the water and measured the depth at 17 fathoms (102 feet; 31 meters). But soon afterwards disaster struck with an ugly scraping sound and a jolting crash. "Before the Man at the lead could heave another cast," Cook later declared, "the ship Struck and stuck fast."

Cook wasted no time responding to this sudden danger. Banks saw him rush onto deck dressed only "in his drawers" at the head of his startled crew. Calmly the captain called out orders and his sailors swiftly obeyed. Some men took in the sails, while others stared into the water tracing the location of the reef. In the ship's boats, crewmen rowed a distance from the *Endeavour* dropping anchors and cables. Hauling upon the anchor cables, sailors strained on deck to pull the *Endeavour* free.

After that effort failed, Cook recalled, "we went to work to lighten her as fast as possible which seem'd to be the only means we had left to get her off." The tons of stones kept in the hull to keep the ship evenly

A coral reef in the Pacific

balanced were hauled up and tossed into the sea. Crewmen next heaved six of the ship's iron cannons overboard. Bundles of firewood, barrels, hoops, staves, and other supplies all splashed into the water.

Although lightened, the *Endeavour* still could not be budged. Through the next day the tide fell and rose again, yet the ship remained stuck fast. Now water leaked into the hull. Deep in the cargo hold, crewmen anxiously worked the ship's pumps hour after hour. The weight and pressure of the ship upon the reef could crack the hull wide open at any time. In the evening of June 12, the tide rose once more. With a sudden lurch, the tilted ship righted itself. Captain Cook seized the moment and ordered his men to grab the anchor cables. Heaving with all their strength, they slowly pulled the *Endeavour* into deep water.

Cook made haste to steer his crippled ship for the Australian coast 30 miles (48 kilometers) away. At the same time, he ordered the hull fothered to slow its leaking. To perform this maneuver, crewmen slapped handfuls of sticky oakum, bits of wool, and sludge onto a spare sail. "The sail thus prepared is hauled under the ship's bottom by ropes," Cook later explained, "and if the place of the leak is uncertain it must be hauled from one part of her bottom to another until the place is found where it takes effect; while the sail is under the ship, the oakum, etc. is washed off and part of it carried along with the water into the leak and in part stops up the hole."

Patched temporarily, the *Endeavour* limped to shore. Sailing along the Australian coast, Cook at last found a shallow inlet, where he beached the ship. Officers and crewmen alike shuddered when they saw the damage the hull had suffered. Four smashed planks left gaping holes. A large piece of coral was still jammed into the worst puncture. Strangely, that hunk of coral had acted as a plug and had kept the ship from leaking faster. Immediately Cook set the ship's carpenter and a team of workers to make repairs.

During the next six weeks the crew camped ashore. Banks and Dr. Solander used the opportunity to gather plants and other natural specimens. Sailors also hiked into the woods hunting wild game for food. Lieutenant John Gore shot one odd Australian creature. The British had never seen such an animal before. "The head, neck and shoulders of this Animal," described Cook, "[were] very small in proportion to the other parts; the tail was nearly as long as the body. . . . Its progression is by hopping . . . 7 or 8 feet at each hop

Kangaroo with its baby, called a joey, in its pouch

Australian aborigines with spear and boomerang

upon its hind legs only." The aborigines called these beasts *kangaroos*. While ashore, the sailors also sighted animals such as the wallaby, a type of small kangaroo, and the dingo, a wild dog.

The aborigines remained a mystery. The British noticed that some natives carried curved pieces of wood, which at first they thought might be wooden swords. The aborigines could hurl them through the air and strike down distant wild game. At other times, these *boomerangs* magically swung back in great arcing circles to the feet of their throwers.

Aerial view of Whitsunday Island off the coast of Queensland, Australia, and inside the Great Barrier Reef. This is one of a group of islands that Cook named the Cumberland Islands in 1770.

At last on August 4, 1770, the *Endeavour* left its river harbor. With its hull patched, the ship leaked only an inch (2.5 centimeters) of water an hour now, and the pumps could keep up with that. Raising just a little canvas to catch the breeze, Cook carefully guided the ship northward. Here the Great Barrier Reef drew even closer to the land. For eight days, the *Endeavour* crisscrossed through the sharp, underwater maze of coral. Finally Cook found a passage that allowed him to sail out into the open ocean.

On August 21, the *Endeavour* coasted past Cape York, Australia's northernmost point, and slipped through Endeavour Strait, between Australia and New Guinea. Two days later, Cook landed on little Possession Island. Beneath a waving British flag, he formally claimed for King George the 2,000 miles (3,219 kilometers) of Australian coastline he had charted.

The busy market of Batavia

In battered condition, the *Endeavour* sailed westward and at last reached Batavia (present-day Djakarta) on October 10. The Dutch at this trading settlement on the Indonesian island of Java welcomed the British sailors. In the harbor, the ship's carpenter replaced rotted planking discovered on the *Endeavour*'s hull. Crewmen also fixed worn sails and frazzled ropes.

At Batavia the British enjoyed their first contact with European civilization in over two years. Unfortunately, the town was not a healthful place to stay. Clouds of mosquitoes bred in nearby swamps carried malaria. Impure drinking water caused dysentery. The British had arrived in excellent health, but before long nearly the entire crew had fallen sick. Surgeon Monkhouse died and so did the Tahitian, Tupia. Illness claimed the lives of five other crewmen before the ship was able to escape Batavia on December 26.

Sick and feverish, Cook's weary men sailed westward across the Indian Ocean to the Cape of Good Hope on Africa's southern tip. During the difficult journey home, twenty-three more crew members died of their Batavia diseases. Sadly Cook watched astronomer Charles Green, artist Sydney Parkinson, and ship's carpenter John Satterly sewn into weighted canvas bags and dropped to watery graves.

After rounding the Cape of Good Hope, the *Endeavour* bounded northward through the Atlantic in fine weather. Several times, the *Endeavour* sailed close to merchant ships on this well traveled ocean. Captains shouted news and questions across the waves. They expressed surprise at discovering the *Endeavour* still afloat after so long an absence at sea. Even now, the Royal Navy ship faced astonishing difficulties. As it neared the end of its voyage, Cook wrote in his journal, "Rigging and sails are now so bad that something or other is giving way every day."

At last, fishermen and sailing crews in the English Channel looked up from their work and stared with surprise and excitement. The *Endeavour* staggered its last few miles home and anchored in a spot called The Downs on July 13, 1771. The *London Evening Post* noted the arrival of "Captain Cooke, from the East Indies" after a voyage of over twenty-two months.

British scientists welcomed Joseph Banks back to England with the highest praise. They eagerly examined the huge collection of plants, animals, and minerals Banks and his assistants had brought home. The specimens included 1,300 flowers never seen before in Europe. The drawings, descriptions, and careful records kept by the *Endeavour*'s naturalists greatly advanced England's knowledge of the world.

Captain Cook received attention, too—from the public, the Lords of the Admiralty, and even King George III. Not long after landing, Cook proudly wrote to his old Whitby friend John Walker: "I had the honor of an hour's conference with the King the other day." Cook presented the Admiralty a detailed report of the *Endeavour*'s travels. "Altho' the discoveries made in this Voyage are not great," he modestly explained, "yet I flatter myself they are such as may Merit the Attention of the Lordships."

In truth, Cook's successful journey had produced many stunning results. His experiments to prevent scurvy caused a great sensation. Cook had shown that clean living conditions and a healthful diet would ward off the dreaded disease. He had not lost a single man to scurvy. Now ships could safely remain at sea for long periods without endangering their crews.

The vast distances sailed by the *Endeavour* earned Cook a place among the world's great explorers. His careful charts filled in many portions of the Pacific map. Geographers now realized the Southern Continent did not lie where they expected. Thanks to Cook, however, 5,000 miles (8,047 kilometers) of Pacific coastline could be found easily. Future British colonists on New Zealand and Australia would owe Cook a great debt of gratitude.

The Royal Navy rewarded Cook with a promotion to the rank of commander. At his Mile End home, the forty-three-year-old sailor embraced his wife and children and considered his feats in the South Pacific. "Little remains now to be done to have a thorough knowledge of that part of the Globe," he declared.

Before long, James Cook would be given the chance to fill in more pieces of the great Pacific puzzle.

Chapter 6
The Resolution and
the Adventure

Commander Cook walked along the docks of the Deptford Navy Yard and gazed with satisfaction at his new ship, HMS *Resolution*. Following the success of Cook's first Pacific voyage, the Lords of the Admiralty immediately began plans for a second. Cook suggested that the new expedition explore the South Atlantic, South Indian, and South Pacific oceans. Using Queen Charlotte's Sound in New Zealand and Matavai Bay in Tahiti as cold-weather bases, Cook wished to venture during warm weather into the unexplored waters around Antarctica. Lord Sandwich, First Lord of the Admiralty, eagerly supported this bold proposal.

The *Endeavour* was not available for this second voyage. It was already engaged carrying cargo to the Falkland Islands. Instead, Royal Navy officers purchased two new Whitby coalships for the expedition: the *Resolution* and the *Adventure*. The *Adventure* measured 97 feet (30 meters) in length. At Woolrich Navy Yard, ship's carpenters converted the merchant ship for Royal Navy service. At the same time, workmen hammered the 111-foot (34-meter) *Resolution* into shape at Deptford Navy Yard. Cook chose the sturdy, stable *Resolution* for his flagship. It was "the properest ship for the service she is intended for of any I ever saw," he remarked with pride.

Joseph Banks expected to join this second expedition. The size of the *Resolution* displeased him, however. He insisted on large, comfortable cabins for himself and his party of twelve naturalists, artists, and servants. At his own expense, Banks ordered the *Resolution* rebuilt to satisfy him. Carpenters sawed planks and raised the deck so that the ship's great cabin would have the headroom Banks wanted. Other new cabins were nailed together on the deck itself, further ruining the vessel's shape.

"I can not answer for her," exclaimed the pilot assigned to guide the *Resolution* down the Thames River. "She'll fall over." Every ripple of water threatened to tip the top-heavy ship. Veteran sailors gaped at the sight and agreed she would never survive a day at sea. Yet Banks turned furious when the Lords of Admiralty wisely ordered the *Resolution* restored to its original, well-balanced condition. Unable to have things his way, Banks withdrew from the expedition.

The Admiralty found replacements to travel with Cook. Two Germans, Johann Reinhold Forster and his son George, signed on as naturalists. Joining them was landscape painter William Hodges, who loaded crates of canvas, paints, pens, and paper onto the *Resolution*. Perhaps most important of all were William Wales and William Bayly. These two astronomers were assigned the duty of determining longitude during the journey.

For centuries, sailors had been able to calculate their latitude, or north-south position, at sea. They found it impossible to calculate their longitude, or east-west position, however. For this, they needed to know the exact difference between the time of day at their ship's position and the time at a fixed point on

John Harrison's first marine chronometer, or sea clock, completed in 1735

shore. As the need to establish longitude grew more urgent, kings of Spain, Holland, and Great Britain offered huge rewards to whoever invented an accurate method.

Finally, in 1735, Englishman John Harrison invented a seagoing clock called a chronometer. This remarkable clock kept nearly perfect time under rough sea conditions and in all climates. Aboard the *Resolution* and the *Adventure*, Cook carried four copies of Harrison's chronometer. Though his ships would range far and wide during the coming voyage, Cook would be the first ship's commander in history to know his exact position on the globe every mile of the way.

The crew of the *Resolution* numbered 110 men. Twenty of these faithful seamen had sailed aboard the *Endeavour*. The smaller *Adventure* carried a crew of eighty men. That vessel would be commanded by Lieutenant Tobias Furneaux, who had sailed around the world aboard the *Dolphin* with Captain Wallis.

Through the last days of spring 1772, laborers loaded the two ships with the vast array of supplies needed for the long voyage. Below the decks, they crowded tons of biscuits, flour, and salted beef and pork. They hefted aboard hundreds of bushels of peas, wheat, and malt, sacks of salt and sugar, and nets of ripe cheese. Cook insisted, of course, on bringing foods that would prevent scurvy. They included 15 tons (13 metric tons) of sauerkraut and 52 gallons (197 liters) of marmalade of carrots.

Cook's ship HMS Resolution

As the time approached for departure, Lord Sandwich honored Cook with a visit aboard the *Resolution*. His position as First Lord of the Admiralty allowed Sandwich to help promote Cook's career. But he has become better know in history for creating the sandwich. According to legend, Lord Sandwich loved gambling so much that he seldom left the gaming tables to eat his meals. Instead, he formed a habit of simply gobbling down a slice of beef slapped between two slices of bread.

At last on July 13, 1772, sailors on the *Resolution* and the *Adventure* hauled up anchor cables. Sails and pennants fluttered and the two ships glided from Plymouth Harbor. At the Madeira and the Cape Verde islands off the African coast, Cook stopped to gather fresh water and supplies. On October 30, the ships reached the southern tip of Africa and put into Cape Town harbor. "At the time we have not one man on the Sick list," Cook proudly wrote. While supplies were loaded aboard, he granted his crews brief shore leaves in the southern African town. There the Forsters met a young Swedish scientist named Anders Sparrman, and Cook invited him to join the expedition.

The end of November found the *Resolution* and the *Adventure* pounding southward through the South Atlantic waves. Winter in the Northern Hemisphere is the warmest season in the Southern Hemisphere. Nevertheless, as Cook steered toward Antarctica, the ships ploughed through storms of sleet and snow.

Through fields of floating ice, the two ships weaved east and west in search of land. The work of sailing in strong gales and thick fogs tested the skills of every crewman. Rain froze in the sailors' hair and beards, while icy gusts turned their bare fingers stiff.

Pack ice of Antarctica

The maze of icebergs grew closer on all sides. Some jutted sixty feet (eighteen meters) in height and measured two miles (3.2 kilometers) around. "It is a general received opinion," Cook penned in his journal, "that ice is formed near land; if so, then there must be land in the neighborhood of this ice." On January 17, the *Resolution* and the *Adventure* crossed the Antarctic Circle. No ships had ever traveled so far south. Another 75 miles (121 kilometers) and Cook would have reached the frozen continent of Antarctica, but too much ice blocked the way. Islands of ice floated so close that they threatened to crush the ships. For safety, Cook turned back toward the northeast.

Hazy weather and dense fog often slowed the progress of the two ships. Finally, on February 9, the *Resolution* lost sight of the *Adventure* completely. Cook

Eighteenth-century chart of the Southern Hemisphere, showing the course Cook's ships took in search of the Southern Continent

and Lieutenant Furneaux had agreed to meet at Queen Charlotte's Sound, New Zealand, if their ships became separated. After one last attempt to sail south beyond the pack ice of the Antarctic Circle, Cook started the *Resolution* toward New Zealand.

Heavy seas washed over the ship's deck and biting winds whipped through its sails. Through the month of March the *Resolution* plowed across the South Indian Ocean. At last, on March 26, 11,000 miles (17,702 kilometers) and 117 days after leaving Cape Town, the *Resolution* entered Dusky Bay on New Zealand's southwest coast. "My first care after the Ship was moored," explained Cook, "was to send a Boat & People fishing." Some sailors landed on a nearby rock and killed a seal. Its meat provided the crew with their first fresh meal in many days.

Through the next weeks the seamen hunted in the woods and collected firewood and fresh water. Battered by its windy journey through the ice, the *Resolution* needed repairs. Some men chopped trees for new planks and spars. Others sewed rips in damaged sails. At last Cook felt ready to haul up the anchor. The *Resolution* scudded north along the island's western coast to Queen Charlotte's Sound.

Lookouts perched in the rigging of the *Resolution* cheered as dawn's early light streaked across the entrance of Queen Charlotte's Sound on May 18, 1773. In the distance stood the outline of the *Adventure* resting at anchor. The *Adventure* had visited Tasmania, an island south of Australia, after its separation from the *Resolution*. Then it had sailed on to Queen Charlotte's Sound, where it had been waiting for six weeks.

Unhappily, Cook discovered that Lieutenant Furneaux had failed to enforce strict rules aboard his ship. Because of unclean conditions and poor diets, about twenty of the *Adventure*'s crew lay ill with scurvy. Already one man had died. Immediately Cook ordered Furneaux to feed his sailors fresh foods, herb juices, and cabbage. Cook personally rowed ashore to pick wild celery and other vegetables for the *Adventure*'s stricken men.

While the sick men were being nursed back to health, Cook visited with the Maori natives ashore. He planted gardens with seeds brought from England. He also presented the natives with some sheep, goats, and pigs he had carried along. The sheep soon died after eating leaves from a poisonous bush. The Maoris quickly ate all the goats, but the pigs at least thrived in the New Zealand woods.

Lieutenant Furneaux had planned to spend the cold summer months snugly anchored in Queen Charlotte's Sound. Captain Cook refused to agree to such idleness, however. Early in June, sails were unfurled and both ships headed eastward. Cook intended to sweep his little fleet back and forth through the South Pacific in an effort to find the Southern Continent if it existed. For six weeks the two ships crossed the stormy seas between the latitudes of 41 degrees and 46 degrees south.

After a second outbreak of scurvy aboard the *Adventure*, Cook ordered his ships north toward the lush vegetation of Tahiti. On August 14, sharp eyes spied Tahiti's green mountains rising on the northern horizon. That night, while Cook slept, his crews mistakenly steered straight ahead. By daylight it was clear the two ships had sailed too close to the reef that guarded the island's southern coast. Stepping up on deck, Captain Cook instantly saw the danger.

"Lee force brace! Down helm!" he shouted. "Bring her up to the wind."

Sailors scrambled into the rigging at the sound of these commands. The helmsmen tried to steer clear, but there was no wind to fill the sails. "None but a seaman can realize how terrible was the sound of waves breaking on the coral reef so near to us," declared Anders Sparrman afterwards. Sparrman recalled that Captain Cook "stamped about the deck and grew hoarse with shouting." Quick action saved both the *Resolution* and the *Adventure* from shipwreck.

When the ships finally anchored at Tahiti's Matavai Bay, smiling natives paddled close and shouted welcomes. Their canoes were piled high with such things

Tahiti's Matavai Bay

as bananas, apples, and coconuts. "The fruits we got here," Cook revealed, "contributed greatly toward the recovery of the *Adventure*'s sick, many of whom were so weak when we put in as not to be able to get on deck without assistance."

Tahiti had changed somewhat since Cook's last visit. Wars among the islanders had killed some natives. Disease left by a ship of visiting Spaniards had killed others. Still, Cook recognized many old friends. While the crews traded nails and bits of iron for hogs and vegetables, the Tahitians continued their cheerful habit of trying to steal anything they could put their hands upon. On one occasion they stripped Anders Sparrman of all of his clothes.

On September 2, 1773, the British ships left Matavai Bay and sailed westward to Huahine, another of the Society Islands. The crews enjoyed two weeks among the happy natives of that island. When the time arrived for parting, one islander named Omai begged to go along. Lieutenant Furneaux invited the sturdy young man aboard the *Adventure*. Out of curiosity, he decided to take Omai to England and expose him to European civilization.

From the Society Islands, Cook sailed his little exploration fleet westward. The Dutchman Tasman claimed to have found islands in that region in 1643, and the Tahitians told Cook that islands did indeed exist in that direction. On October 2, Cook rediscovered the Tonga Islands. That evening the *Resolution* and the *Adventure* anchored, and pulleys creaked as ships' boats were lowered into the water.

Cook, Furneaux, and their boat crews received an overwhelming greeting as they neared the shore. Native men and women thronged the beach shouting welcomes to the strangers. "They crowded so thick around the boats," Cook later exclaimed, "with Cloth, Matting, etc. to exchange for Nails that it was some time before we could get room to land."

During their stay, the British received such endless gifts of fruit and vegetables that the coconuts, bananas, lemons, sugarcanes, and other foods stood in great mounds upon the ships' decks. The natives showed so much joy and good cheer day after day that Cook renamed the Tonga Islands the Friendly Islands. Many of the sailors on the *Resolution* and the *Adventure* would have been happy to stay forever. On October 7, 1773, however, Cook ordered sails hoisted. The warm season was approaching and it was time again to head toward the Antarctic.

Levuka, one of the Tonga Islands

Chapter 7
"Room for Very Large Islands"

Sheets of rain slashed at decks and sails. Cruel winds pitched the two British ships awkwardly through mountains of foaming waves. For days the *Resolution* and the *Adventure* tumbled toward New Zealand through heavy squalls until, on the night of October 30, 1773, they lost contact with each other.

Captain Cook steered the *Resolution* onward to New Zealand. He expected to find the *Adventure* again at their regular meeting place in Queen Charlotte's Sound. While the *Resolution*'s crew collected supplies, Cook waited. By the end of three weeks, however, he paced in his cabin impatiently. If he waited any longer, he would miss the best weather for Antarctic exploration. Beneath a tree in the cove, he buried a message sealed in a bottle for Lieutenant Furneaux. On the tree he carved the words "Look Underneath." The following day, November 25, the *Resolution* left Queen Charlotte's Sound and headed south into the uncharted South Pacific.

Six days later, the *Adventure* finally straggled into Queen Charlotte's Sound. It was too late to try to catch up with the *Resolution*. Furneaux rested his weary crewmen and repaired his storm-battered ship. A clash with the fierce Maori ended horribly for one shore party of British soldiers. The natives attacked the boat, killed eleven men, and roasted their bodies for a cannibal feast. Soon afterwards, the *Adventure* sailed for home. The ship journeyed round South America's Cape Horn, crossed north through the Atlantic, and arrived in England in July 1774. As a result, Tobias Furneaux became the first explorer to sail around the world following a west-to-east route.

Meanwhile, the *Resolution* cut a lonely path searching for land in the wide South Pacific. During the month of December 1773, the ship fought its way through fogs, gales, and blizzards. After crossing the Antarctic Circle, the *Resolution*'s crew celebrated Christmas in the midst of a snowstorm. "Snow . . . froze to the rigging as it fell," recalled Cook, "and decorated the whole with icicles. Our ropes were like wires, Sails like board or plates of Metal." Icebergs, ghostly and jagged, crowded the freezing water. Naturalist Johann Forster declared, "the whole scene looks like the wreck of a shattered world."

At the end of January 1774, the *Resolution* reached the latitude of 71 degrees, 10 minutes—more than four degrees inside the Antarctic Circle. This was as far south as Cook or anyone else had ever sailed. Here great mountains of ice blocked any further progress. "I who had Ambition not only to go Farther than anyone had done before, but as far as it was possible for man to go, was not sorry at meeting with this interruption," admitted Cook. He correctly guessed

Maori carved clubs

that land lay beyond the frozen southern horizon. Unable to reach it, however, he gladly steered the *Resolution* toward warmer water to the north.

Cook's orders permitted him to return to England now if he chose. But he decided first to explore more of the South Pacific, "for although I had proved there was no continent," he wrote in his journal, "there remained, nevertheless, room for very large islands." For weeks the *Resolution* bounded northward. The empty ocean sparkled green in all directions and the west wind slapped the little vessel's sails. During much of this time, Cook lay deathly ill with stomach cramps in his cabin. Years of sailors' food and the strain of command had finally caught up with him. His loyal crew slowly nursed him back to health with the aid of a dog-meat broth, the only fresh meat aboard, prepared by Johann Forster.

At last on March 23, 1774, after 103 days at sea, the *Resolution* reached land. Jacob Roggeveen had discovered Easter Island in 1722, and Cook had read an account of that Dutch explorer's voyage. As the *Resolution* neared shore, Cook and his sailors saw great carved stone heads standing on the hillsides, and they knew they had come to Easter Island.

The natives of Easter Island greeted their visitors with friendliness. The soil, however, was parched and dry and food was scarce. "There is hardly an island in this sea," unhappily commented Cook, "which affords less refreshments. . . . Nature has hardly provided it with anything fit for man to eat or drink." While his men traded trinkets for potatoes, sugarcane, and a few other supplies, Captain Cook curiously walked among the island's stone head monuments. The reason for these giant statues was a mystery. The na-

Stone figures of Easter Island

tives did not seem to worship them as religious symbols. Cook guessed they were used as burial markers.

After its brief stop at Easter Island, the *Resolution* pushed on for Tahiti. On April 22, the familiar green mountains of Matavai Bay loomed into view. The bay appeared very different than it had on previous visits. More than three hundred large war canoes stood massed together on the water. The 60- to 80-foot (18- to 24-meter) vessels, Cook observed, "were decorated with Flags, Streamers, etc. so that the whole made a grand and Noble appearance such as was never seen before in this Sea." Aboard, some eight thousand warriors in colorful robes, turbans, and feathered helmets were equipped with paddles, clubs, and spears.

Cook learned that this war fleet had been assembled for an attack against unfriendly chiefs on the nearby island of Moorea. While the *Resolution* lay anchored in the bay, the Tahitian war fleet demonstrated its skill. In response to shouted commands, warriors dug their paddles into the water. The canoes dashed forward in difficult and impressive patterns. "I must confess," Cook wrote afterwards, "I would willingly have stayed five days longer had I been sure the expedition would then take place, but it rather seem'd that they wanted us to be gone first."

Respectful of the Tahitians' wishes, the British sailed away without witnessing the sea battle. Through the next days the *Resolution* visited among others of the Society and Friendly Islands. At last on June 4, Cook noted that he and his crew "took our final leave of these happy isles and the Good People in them." Cook's curiosity drew the *Resolution* westward. He wished to explore the New Hebrides Islands, first discovered by Pedro de Queiros in 1606.

This volcano on Tanna Island in the New Hebrides has been active for four hundred years.

Six weeks of South Pacific winds blew the *Resolution* to the New Hebrides. Here, for the first time in the Pacific, Cook encountered black-skinned natives. These people wore bracelets studded with shells on their arms and feathers in their kinky black hair. The shells and feathers they gladly traded for pieces of cloth and medals engraved with King George's face.

From the New Hebrides Cook sailed south, and in September he chanced upon a long island never before discovered. He named it New Caledonia. Shy natives visited aboard the *Resolution*, and Cook gave them gifts of nails and pieces of red cloth. "They were curious to look into every corner of the Ship," he later wrote. Everything aboard the strange vessel struck these simple people full of wonder.

Through difficult seas the *Resolution* continued southward. Cook wished to stop in New Zealand and gather supplies before heading for home. The ship discovered little Norfolk Island before coasting into Queen Charlotte's Sound on October 18, 1774. Cook saw signs that the *Adventure* had visited there. The message in the bottle he had buried was missing. Fresh tree stumps showed that timber had been cut for ship masts. He would not learn of the cannibal attack on Furneaux's sailors, however, until months later. For three weeks Cook's men overhauled the *Resolution* and refreshed themselves.

As winter warmth returned to the waters of the South Pacific, the *Resolution* started homeward with wind-puffed sails. Following the 55-degree-south latitude, the British ship journeyed more than 8,000 miles (12,874 kilometers) eastward without sighting any land. At last the *Resolution* neared the coast of South America in the middle of December. With relief

Rock formation seen from the island of New Caledonia

and pride, Cook penned in his journal, "I have now done with the SOUTHERN PACIFIC OCEAN. I hope . . . no one will think that I have left it unexplored or that more could have been done in one voyage."

The *Resolution* spent its third Christmas on the rocky shores of Tierra del Fuego. The crew feasted on the ship's last bottles of wine and "goose pie" made with local seabirds. During the following days, the explorers sailed the dangerous waters around Cape Horn so that Cook could carefully chart the region on his maps. The new year of 1775 found the *Resolution* plunging eastward through the icy waves of the South Atlantic. On January 20, crewmen spied a small island whose mountains were covered with snow. Populated by barking seals and waddling penguins, Cook named the place South Georgia in honor of King George III. When the *Resolution* later chanced upon two other small, frigid islands, Cook named them the South Sandwich Islands after Lord Sandwich.

The hardy crew of the *Resolution* saw no other land on its journey across 5,000 miles (8,047 kilometers) of the South Atlantic. Once more Cook guessed that, if land existed, it lay farther south near the pole. Whoever had the strength and daring to reach that frozen region, Cook declared, "I shall not envy him the honour of the discovery."

On March 21, 1775, the *Resolution* reached Africa's Cape of Good Hope, thus completing a full circle around the globe. In the Dutch harbor of Cape Town, the explorers enjoyed their first tastes of European-style civilization in two-and-a-half years. Damaged rigging on the *Resolution* required repairs, but the ship remained in good shape otherwise. After a five-week stay, Cook continued the voyage home.

Snow-covered mountains of South Georgia, which Cook named after King George III

The *Resolution* steered north through the Atlantic, stopping at the islands of St. Helena, Ascension, and the Azores along the way. Perched high in the rigging, sailors finally waved and pointed to a joyful sight on July 29, 1775. It was the southern coast of England. The next day, after an incredible voyage that had lasted three years and eighteen days, the ship dropped anchor in Portsmouth Harbor.

Throughout Great Britain, messengers and newspapers excitedly trumpeted word of James Cook's successful return. Among the remarkable achievements of his second expedition, Cook had discovered new islands and rediscovered many forgotten ones. With the help of his chronometers, he had charted his route with total accuracy.

For the first time, European geographers possessed a clear picture of the South Pacific. Cook had proven once and for all that no fertile Southern Continent existed in the world.

He had also proven without a doubt the proper methods for preventing scurvy aboard ship. During the *Resolution*'s three long years at sea, four sailors had died: three by accidents and one by a disease other than scurvy. Thanks to Cook's dietary rules, not a single man had died of scurvy.

A coach carried Cook over rutted dirt roads to London, where King George III welcomed him. Common Britons drank toasts and cheered the greatest explorer in their nation's history.

Because of his scientific work against scurvy, Cook earned the Copley Gold Medal. This was highest award granted by the Royal Society. The Royal Society also elected Cook as a member of their highly respected group.

The Royal Navy honored Cook with a promotion to the rank of post-captain. In addition, the Lords of the Admiralty rewarded him with an appointment as captain of His Majesty's Royal Hospital for Seamen at Greenwich.

Cook's position as head of this Royal Navy hospital for retired sailors paid well and demanded little attention. It seemed that, at the age of forty-seven, Cook was being invited to relax and enjoy his worldwide fame.

Captain Cook

Chapter 8
The Third Pacific Voyage

"My fate drives me from one extreme to another," James Cook wrote to his old friend John Walker in the summer of 1775. *"A few months ago the whole Southern Hemisphere was hardly big enough for me, and now I am going to be confined to the limits of Greenwich Hospital, which are far too small for an active mind like mine."*

At Greenwich Hospital, Cook performed his easy duties and spent some time editing the journal of his second voyage for publication. His spectacular record during nearly thirty years of service at sea had earned Cook the right to stay at home. But it soon became clear that the great explorer was bored with life on land.

At the Admiralty, plans were being drawn for another major Pacific voyage. For centuries Europeans had tried to find a northern sea route from the Atlantic Ocean to the Pacific Ocean. Thoughts of a "Northwest Passage"—a shorter course than the Cape of Good Hope and Cape Horn routes—excited sea merchants. Such a route would save them time in reaching the rich trading centers of China and India. While exploring the eastern coast of North America, Henry Hudson, Martin Frobisher, William Baffin, and others had failed to find the fabled passage. Much of North America's western coast, however, remained totally unmapped.

Vitus Bering's search for a land connection between Asia and North America ended in shipwreck.

Sir Francis Drake

English adventurer Francis Drake had touched upon the western coast briefly during his round-the-world cruise in 1579. Spanish and Russian navigators also had sailed into the region without gaining much more information. After 1728, the English heard reports that a Danish seaman named Vitus Bering, sailing for Russia, had discovered a narrow strait separating Asia and North America. This raised hopes that a wide passage existed across the top of the world. In 1745, the British government eagerly offered a prize of twenty thousand pounds to the explorer who discovered such a route.

Having sent expeditions in the past, the Admiralty now decided to try again. In February 1776, Captain Cook sat at a dinner party that included Lord Sandwich, Sir Hugh Palliser, and Sir Philip Stephens, secretary of the Admiralty. Cook listened as the men discussed the problems of organizing the coming voyage. They wondered who among their officers could command such a difficult journey. On the spur of the moment, Cook jumped to his feet. Excitedly he volunteered to command the expedition himself.

Within a few days, the Lords of Admiralty formally accepted his generous offer. Cook's pen flew across paper as he soon announced in a happy letter to John Walker, "I have quitted an easy retirement for an active, perhaps dangerous voyage." Cook deserved at least a longer rest. Having conquered the South Pacific, however, he could think of nothing but getting back to sea and conquering the North Pacific, too.

The Admiralty had already chosen HMS *Resolution* for duty on this expedition. In truth, though, after three years of South Seas heat and Antarctic ice, the ship was no longer in good sailing condition. At Deptford Navy Yard, shipworkers scurried about refitting masts, refilling seams with caulk, and replacing the ropes in the rigging. At the time, dozens of ships floated side by side in the yard, all demanding attention. A revolution had erupted in the American colonies, and the Royal Navy was preparing for war. As a result, the Deptford shipworkers rushed their pace, cut corners, and in general did a poor, dishonest job in overhauling the *Resolution*. The Admiralty bought another Whitby coalship to accompany the *Resolution*. At 298 tons, the little *Discovery* would prove the sturdier of the two.

Thirty-three-year-old Lieutenant Charles Clerke received command of HMS *Discovery*. Clerke was the one officer who had sailed on both of Cook's previous voyages. Other skilled officers and men also joined the expedition, many simply for the honor of serving under Captain Cook. First lieutenant aboard the *Resolution* was forty-six-year-old John Gore, who had sailed on the *Endeavour*. Cook chose twenty-one-year-old William Bligh to be master aboard the *Resolution*. Several years later, as commander of his own ship, Captain Bligh would survive a famous mutiny on the *Bounty*. Signed on as a midshipman, or apprentice officer, was fourteen-year-old George Vancouver. In 1792, Vancouver would lead his own expedition into the North Pacific and make a name for himself. The

George Vancouver

Cook's ship HMS Discovery

Adventure's astronomer, William Bayly, prepared to sail again, and ship's surgeon William Anderson expected to serve also as naturalist of the expedition. Swiss artist John Webber agreed to ship aboard and draw a record of his observations. Altogether, the *Resolution* would possess a crew of 112 and the *Discovery* would carry 70.

King George III suggested that Cook carry supplies of vegetable seeds and some livestock as gifts to the natives of the Society and Friendly islands. "Took on board a Bull, 2 Cows, with their Calves and some sheep," noted Cook on June 10, 1776. These and other animals so crowded the *Resolution* that Cook joked that his ship was "a Noah's Ark."

Seagulls glided in the sky over Plymouth Harbor on July 12, 1776. With eager shouts, sailors turned the capstan and hauled up the *Resolution*'s anchor cable. Then the ship bounded out into the waves of the English Channel. The *Discovery* would follow afterwards and join the *Resolution* at Cape Town.

As the *Resolution* sailed into the open sea, one passenger stood on deck very proudly dressed in fancy English clothes. For two years, the South Pacific native Omai had lived in London society. As a guest of Sir Joseph Banks, Omai had dined with noblemen and had attended the opera. His brown skin and long hair had attracted interest wherever he went. As he learned English, Omai had amused Londoners with his witty and charming comments on life in Britain. Presented at court to King George III, the simple islander had broken royal formality by saying "How do King Tosh." Now Omai was on his way home. His cabin was jammed with muskets, pistols, a suit of armor, a hand organ, toy soldiers, a globe of the world, and many other English gifts he had received during his stay. He was sure these curious items and his stories of England would impress the people of his islands.

Cook's instructions for his third voyage included stops at New Zealand and Tahiti. Afterwards his ships were expected to enter the North Pacific and sail along the coast of North America. "Search for, and explore, such rivers or inlets as may appear to be of a considerable extent, and pointing towards Hudson's or Baffin's Bays," read the captains orders. If a northern waterway existed between the Pacific and the Atlantic, the Admiralty felt certain that James Cook, of all men, would be able to find it.

The English Channel near Whitby

The *Resolution*'s journey south to Cape Town revealed the shoddy work of the Deptford Navy Yard. Caulking popped out of seams, causing the ship to leak. Under the pressure of wind and sail, the mizzenmast cracked and could no longer be used.

After the *Resolution* arrived at Cape Town, Cook and his crew spent three busy weeks making repairs. By the time Lieutenant Clerke and the *Discovery* reached the harbor, the *Resolution* had been overhauled as well as possible. Together the two ships turned out to sea on November 30.

Through days of thick fog, the *Resolution* and the *Discovery* steered into the South Indian Ocean. To keep in touch, they fired signal guns from time to time.

The ships stopped at a few small islands recently discovered by the French. On December 24, 1776, Cook sighted barren Kerguelen Island and anchored his ships at a place he called Christmas Harbor. Cook wrote that he saw plenty of "Seals, Penguins and other birds on the shore but not a stick of wood." For several days the British explored the cold, rocky island before sailing onward.

Bad luck followed Cook into the new year of 1777. In the midst of a storm, roaring winds tore away the topmast of the *Resolution*. Rigging, sails, and spars crashed down onto the deck. Cook sailed for Tasmania in order to fix the damage. Anchored at Adventure Bay, where Furneaux had stopped four years before, Cook began his first and only visit to that island on January 26. At Adventure Bay, sailors chopped tall trees for masts and spare timber, sawed brush for firewood, and gathered green grass to feed the ships' livestock.

One afternoon, Cook later remembered, "we were agreeably surprised at the place where we were cutting Wood, with a visit from some of the Natives, Eight men and a boy: they came out of the Woods to us without showing the least mark of fear . . . none of them had any weapons. . . . They were quite naked and wore no ornaments." Gentle and cheerful, the Tasmanian natives showed hardly any curiosity about their British visitors.

After stocking the ships with wood, grass, and water, Cook sailed on to New Zealand. On February 11, heavy ships' anchors once again splashed in Queen Charlotte's Sound. The Maori murderers of Lieutenant Furneaux's boat crew feared the return of the British. Captain Cook, however chose to keep the peace rather than seek revenge.

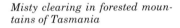

Misty clearing in forested mountains of Tasmania

After a brief stay of just two weeks, Cook continued his voyage. He realized he could not delay if he wished to reach the Arctic in summer weather. But the trade winds between New Zealand and Tahiti refused to assist Cook with his plans. For weeks, no more than the lightest breeze touched their sails as the *Resolution* and the *Discovery* slowly floated over the ocean's glassy surface.

The ships passed among some new discoveries, a small island group that later became known as the Cook Islands. Curious natives flocked along the shores, but Cook saw no easy place to anchor. Aboard deck the noise of bleating goats and mooing cows reminded the captain he must soon find fresh grass and water for his livestock. Turning west, he steered his ships toward the Friendly Islands.

At the end of April, joyous natives greeted the British at the Friendly Island of Nomuka. The sailors herded the livestock ashore to munch on lush tropical grasses. Setting up a marketplace, the crewmen traded glass beads, cloth, and nails for fat pigs, coconuts, breadfruit, yams, and bananas. From neighboring islands, natives paddled canoes filled with more food for trade. In no time, the *Resolution* and the *Discovery* were well stocked with fresh and tasty things to eat.

The natural habit of the Friendly Islanders to steal caused Captain Cook some problems. Native thieves stole such things as turkeys, clothes, Lieutenant Clerk's pet cats, and at least one important navigating instrument, a sextant. The British whipped some captured thieves and punished others by shaving their heads. Cook finally settled on one method for recovering stolen property. He held chiefs hostage until the missing things were returned.

Pools beneath a waterfall on one of the Friendly Islands

The need to stop among the Friendly Islands had thrown off Cook's voyage schedule. Rather than push on for the North Atlantic, he now decided to spend most of the rest of 1777 in the tropics. After three months of feasts and such happy native entertainments as dancing, singing, and boxing tournaments, the fattened crews of the *Resolution* and the *Discovery* set sail from the Friendly Islands. It was time to take Omai home to the islands of Tahiti.

A month of sunny skies carried the ships eastward to Tahiti. At last on the morning of August 12, the island rose into view. Aboard the *Resolution*, sailor David Samwell later recalled, "Omai sat all day on the forecastle viewing his Native shores with Tears in his Eyes." Within days the ships anchored in Matavai Bay. Tahitian natives stared in wonder as Omai strutted ashore in his fine European clothes. Captain

The Huahine native Omai

Cook at last cleared the decks of his ships by presenting King George III's gifts of cattle, sheep, ducks, geese, turkeys, and peacocks to island chiefs. To impress his friends, Omai freely handed out many of his curious treasures from England.

During the summer and fall, the two British ships cruised to other islands in the Tahitian chain. Finally Cook returned Omai to his native island of Huahine. Ship's carpenters fitted together a wooden house for Omai, and sailors planted a garden for him with a grapevine, a shaddock tree, pineapples, and melons. Captain Cook gave the young man two horses, a goat, and three pigs. Once Omai was settled in comfort, it was time for the British to leave. With a full heart, Omai said goodbye and watched as the two ships sailed away. He would never see his friend Captain Cook again.

Chapter 9
Northern Discoveries

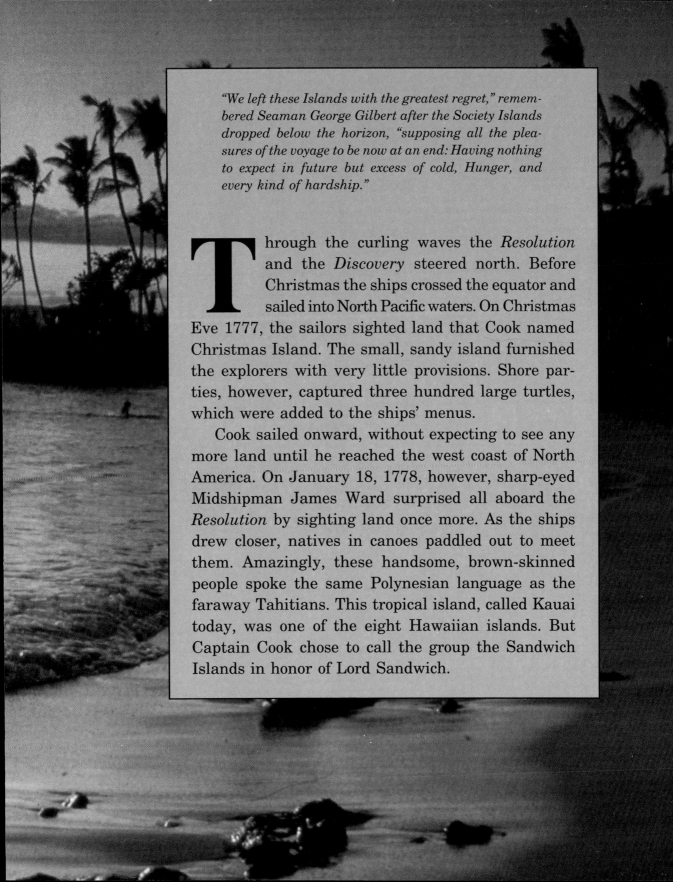

"We left these Islands with the greatest regret," remembered Seaman George Gilbert after the Society Islands dropped below the horizon, "supposing all the pleasures of the voyage to be now at an end: Having nothing to expect in future but excess of cold, Hunger, and every kind of hardship."

Through the curling waves the *Resolution* and the *Discovery* steered north. Before Christmas the ships crossed the equator and sailed into North Pacific waters. On Christmas Eve 1777, the sailors sighted land that Cook named Christmas Island. The small, sandy island furnished the explorers with very little provisions. Shore parties, however, captured three hundred large turtles, which were added to the ships' menus.

Cook sailed onward, without expecting to see any more land until he reached the west coast of North America. On January 18, 1778, however, sharp-eyed Midshipman James Ward surprised all aboard the *Resolution* by sighting land once more. As the ships drew closer, natives in canoes paddled out to meet them. Amazingly, these handsome, brown-skinned people spoke the same Polynesian language as the faraway Tahitians. This tropical island, called Kauai today, was one of the eight Hawaiian islands. But Captain Cook chose to call the group the Sandwich Islands in honor of Lord Sandwich.

Some brave natives climbed aboard the ships. "I never saw Indians so much astonished at entering a ship before," declared Cook; "their eyes were continually flying from object to object." The surprised natives stared at the shiny brass fittings and gently touched the broad white canvas sails. Clearly these people had never seen a ship before. Some simple natives picked up ropes and other wonderful things they saw on deck. They intended to keep them, but the British sailors made them put them back.

As soon as the ships were anchored, Cook rowed ashore in a ship's boat. In front of a village, hundreds of natives crowded the beach. "The very instant I leaped ashore," explained Cook, "they all fell flat on their faces, and remained in that humble posture till I made signs to them to rise." These people quickly brought Cook gifts of small pigs and bowls heaped with colorful fruits and vegetables. Cook guessed that this was the kind of generous treatment they normally showed visiting chiefs.

Through the next day the British easily traded nails and iron for food supplies. The respectful Hawaiians also gladly helped load kegs of fresh water aboard the ships. "They are an open . . . active people and the most expert swimmers we had met with," remarked Captain Cook. Their good nature impressed the explorer and he recognized the importance of these islands, located as they were in the middle of the wide Pacific. After a pleasant stay of two weeks, the British finally hoisted sails and continued their journey north.

Rough weather drove the ships within sight of North America on March 7, 1778. Beginning along the tree-lined shore of present-day Oregon, Cook sailed slowly up the coast. Beaten by high winds and rocking

Alaska's Nootka Sound around the year 1785

waves, by the end of the month the *Resolution* needed crucial repairs. At Vancouver Island, now part of Canada's British Columbia, Cook anchored in a sound known today by its native name Nootka Sound.

The *Resolution*'s mizzenmast had collapsed and sailors noticed rotten wood in the foremast. "It was lucky these defects were discovered in a place where wood . . . was to be had," Cook later exclaimed, "for among the driftwood in the Cove where we lay, were some well seasoned trees and very proper for our purpose, one of which was pitched upon and Carpenters went to work."

Some sailors clipped dead branches from this new mizzenmast, while others found a tall, straight tree in the woods and chopped it down for a foremast. The ship's blacksmith set up a forge and hammered iron fittings for these masts. "As we found the Ship again very leaky in her upper works," Cook also noted, "the Caulkers were set to work to caulk her and repair such other defects as were wanting."

Peaceful Nootka Indians gathered to look at the strange ships and watch the visitors work. Cook described the looks of these North American natives: "Their face is rather broad and flat, with highish cheekbones and plump cheeks. Their mouth is little and round . . . their eyes are black. . . . Their complexion is swarthy." The clothes they wore, made of animal skins and woven tree bark, smelled of smoke and fish. When they paddled close they often sang lovely songs together, keeping rhythm by beating their paddles against the sides of their canoes.

"A great many Canoes filled with Natives were about the Ships all day," remembered Cook, "and a trade commenced betwixt us and them, which was carried on with the strictest honesty on both sides." Among the items the natives offered for trade were furs of the bear, wolf, and fox, as well as beautiful, glossy sea otter pelts. "For these things they took in exchange, Knives, chisels, pieces of iron & Tin, Nails, Buttons, or any kind of metal. Beads they were not fond of and cloth of all kinds they rejected." These shrewd traders also charged the British for the wood and water they collected and the grass they cut for the ships' goats. "There was not a blade of grass that had not a [native] owner," remarked Cook, "so that I very soon emptied my pockets with purchasing."

At the end of April, the *Resolution* and the *Discovery* sailed from Nootka Sound. Farther north, the high mountain peaks along the coast showed Cook that no water passageway would be found there. During the first week of May, the two ships fought rainstorms and heavy seas. Water began leaking through the sides of the *Resolution*'s hull. To fix this latest damage, Cook anchored in a sheltered harbor in a wide gulf he named Prince William Sound, on present-day Alaska's southern coast.

The Eskimo people of this region were different from the Nootka Indians. Their native canoes called *kayaks* were covered over with waterproof skins leaving only one or two holes in which passengers could sit. One British sailor shouted out in surprise upon coming face to face with one of the Prince William Sound natives. He was sure the man had two mouths. Perhaps to frighten enemies, these natives had a tradition of cutting a slit below their lower lip, through which they sometimes poked their tongue.

For several days, sailors caulked the *Resolution*'s leaky seams. Then the ships sailed ahead. On May 28, the two vessels entered a wide opening, which has since been named Cook Inlet. For four days Cook sailed north into the inlet, often sending Master Bligh ahead in a ship's boat to measure the depth of the water. As the waterway grew narrower, Cook correctly guessed he was on a river and not the gateway to any northern passage. Before turning back, he sent two small boats ashore to "take possession of the country and river in His Majesty's name," he explained, "and to bury in the ground a bottle containing two pieces of English coin (date 1772) and a paper on which was inscribed the ships' names, date, etc."

Glacier at Prince William Sound

Fresh, cool breezes pushed the *Resolution* and the *Discovery* farther along the coastline. The ships passed a great island the natives called Kodiak Island. Then instead of turning north, as Cook expected, the coastline led in a southwesterly direction. Through the month of June, Cook sailed along the Alaska Peninsula, with its shoreline of rugged hills and high, rocky cliffs. Days of fog and slashing rain made the work of charting this coastline very difficult. For several days, the ships skirted along the Aleutians before Cook realized they were a chain of islands.

On June 25, Cook steered for an opening between two of the islands, but darkness arrived before he reached it. Blindly, in an inky fog, the ships groped ahead, water rippling against their hulls. In the morning the sailors gasped in horror. During the night they had sailed between two great rocks barely a quarter mile (.4 kilometer) apart. Only luck had saved the ships from crashing. Gratefully Captain Cook named the Aleutian island they had just passed Providence Island, although its natives called it Unalaksa Island.

After passing through the Aleutians, Cook steered into the Bering Sea. The coast of Alaska as it turned northward remained rough and unpredictable. *Resolution* officers sometimes scanned a poorly sketched Russian map Cook possessed, but it gave the sailors little help. "There never was a Map," complained Lieutenant James King, "so unlike what it ought to be." Carefully Cook pressed on, past shoals and jutting points of land. On August 8, 1778, the ships passed the westernmost point of land on the North American mainland. Cook named it Cape Prince of Wales after King George III's first son.

Aleuts of Unalaska Island

Strong winds swept the *Resolution* and the *Discovery* west across the Bering Strait. At its narrowest point, the strait separated Asia and North America by only 55 miles (89 kilometers). Cook needed to be certain this opening led to the Arctic Circle. When sailors spotted a native village on the icy Asian shore, Cook ordered a ship's boat to land him there. Bravely he walked alone toward a group of armed Chuckchi natives. His calm behavior soon gained their confidence. The Chuckchi men placed their weapons on the ground and performed a song and dance of friendship.

Cook noticed that the culture of the Chuckchi was different than that of Alaskan natives. Assured that he had landed upon Asia, Cook mapped a northerly course. For days, the ships dodged through the floating ice of the Arctic Ocean. Often the sailors saw great wallowing walruses. "They lay in herds of many hundreds upon the ice," explained Cook, "and roar or bray very loud, so that in the night or foggy weather they gave us notice of the ice long before we could see it." Rowing close in boats, sailors shot some of these giant beasts. The boiled meat gave the crews something fresh to gnaw upon at mealtimes.

Through the last two weeks of August, the *Resolution* and the *Discovery* crept between crowding icebergs. The danger of crushing ice lurked everywhere. Through thick fog, lookouts strained their eyes for safe passageways. Working the ice-crusted ropes and sails, sailors' fingers turned blue with frostbite. The ships struggled as far as 70 degrees, 44 minutes north latitude until finally, on August 27, a 12-foot (3.7-meter) wall of solid ice loomed ahead.

For two days, Cook sailed back and forth searching for a break in the massive ice field before turning back. The season's warmest weather had ended, and Cook realized he would find no passage that year. "My attention," he explained in his journal, "was now directed towards finding out some place where we could Wood and Water, and in considering how I should spend the Winter. . . . No place was so conveniently within our reach . . . as [the] Sandwich Islands, to these islands, therefore, I intended to proceed."

Back through the Bering Strait and across the Bering Sea, the British ships beat their way southward. Although the *Discovery* seemed sturdy and fine, each day's travel revealed new weaknesses aboard the *Resolution*. Hoping to repair some of the damage, Cook sailed for Unalaska Island.

On October 3, the ships took shelter at a deep harbor called Samgoonoodha. While some men worked upon the *Resolution*, others traded with the Eskimos or fished for salmon. Cook knew that Russian fur traders had established small settlements on many of the Aleutian Islands. One day, several Russians dressed in furs came to visit. They examined Cook's maps of the North Pacific but could give him little help in unlocking the puzzle of the frozen Arctic. After nearly a month on Unalaska, the *Resolution* and the *Discovery* sailed away for warmer weather. The sailors were eager to reach the sunny, beautiful Hawaiian Islands. After a winter of rest and relaxation, Cook planned to try the Arctic again the next year.

Aduk Island, one of Alaska's Aleutian Islands

Chapter 10
Death in the Pacific

Pounding waves and shrieking winds drove the two British ships southward. Aboard the *Discovery* a mast collapsed, killing one man and injuring several others. After this awful storm, another long thirty days of sailing brought the voyagers within sight of the Hawaiian island of Maui on November 26, 1778. Braced against the deck rail of the *Resolution*, Captain Cook gazed through his spyglass. The shore of Maui appeared rocky and steep. No easy harbor lay in sight.

Day after day the ships cruised close to land, searching for safe haven. Past the islands of Maui, Oahu, and Molokai the ships sailed back and forth, taking care to stay free of reefs. Waving natives sometimes ran along the shorelines. Some grinning islanders paddled out to welcome the passing ships. Weary sailors grumbled that it was torture to be so near these beautiful islands and not be able to land.

Finally Cook steered around to the west coast of the largest island in the group, Hawaii. Battered by months at sea, the *Resolution* and the *Discovery* at last limped into a lovely open bay the natives called Kealakekua on January 17, 1779. Along the shore, islanders grabbed paddles and jumped into their wooden canoes. Others splashed out into the water and swam toward the two anchored ships. In no time, cheerful Hawaiians crowded onto the decks. They hung from the anchor cables, clung to the gunports, and nimbly climbed into rigging and sails. Joyful songs and laughter filled the air. Bountiful gifts of pigs, fruit, coconuts, and other fresh foods promised the sailors a delicious change in their diets. After months of frozen ice, tossing seas, and buffeting winds, this incredible Hawaiian welcome seemed like a dream.

Captain Cook soon put his men to work making repairs, gathering wood and water, and trading for food. Always the islanders showed their visitors the greatest possible respect. "It is very clear," observed Lieutenant King, "that they regard us as . . . their superiors." As leader of the strangers, the Hawaiians treated Captain Cook with special attention. The first time Cook stepped ashore, the high priest Koa approached him with solemn ceremony. "He presented me," recalled Cook, "with a small pig, two coconuts and a piece of red cloth which he draped round me." Island chieftains gave Cook valuable gifts and the people bowed low before him wherever he walked.

With good nature, Cook twice allowed Koa and another native priest named Kili'ikea to lead him through long religious rituals. The natives called him "Rono," but he hardly guessed that they believed he was the Hawaiian god of peace and happiness. By a

Cook being greeted by natives of the Sandwich Islands

strange twist of fate, however, Cook and his amazing ships seemed to fulfill much of Rono's ancient legend.

For two weeks, the awed people of Kealakekua Bay treated the British strangers with the deepest respect. At great feasts, the two hundred sailors happily gobbled the food placed before them. Soon, though, the natives clearly had little more to give. With his ships fairly well repaired, Cook decided to visit among the neighboring islands.

With bright smiles and sighs of relief, the Hawaiians wished their guests good-bye on February 4. They watched the strangers open the great white banners that hung in the "trees" on their ships and sail out of the bay. The god Rono had expected much from them, and they were glad to see him go.

With happy memories and full stomachs, the British sailors headed straight into a tropical storm. On the night of February 7, the *Resolution* pitched through the water so roughly that its foremast cracked and sprang from the deck. Only the ropes of the rigging held it upright. Cook knew he must find a harbor immediately. Reluctantly he gave the order to turn back to Kealakekua Bay.

The ships sailed back into the bay on February 11. The sailors expected to find flocks of joyful Hawaiians waiting on the beaches. "Upon our coming to anchor," remarked Lieutenant King, "we were surprised to find our reception very different from what it had been on our first arrival; no shouts, no bustle, no confusion; but a solitary bay, with only here and there a canoe stealing close along the shore."

Early map showing the major islands of Hawaii

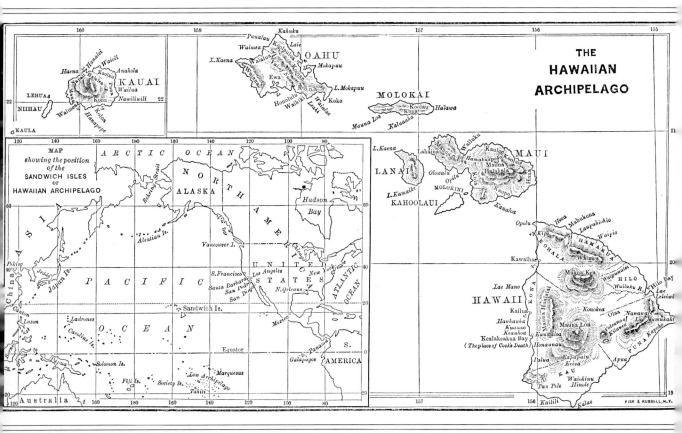

The natives had already given away so much of their food. Now it appeared that Rono had returned to demand even more. Unhappily they watched as workers took down the *Resolution*'s damaged mast and floated it to shore for repairs. Some islanders refused to help crewmen sent ashore to fill water barrels. Other resentful natives swam out to the ships and stole nails by prying them from the hulls.

Tensions increased on the afternoon of February 13. While Lieutenant Clerke entertained a chieftain named Parea in his cabin on the *Discovery*, a Hawaiian climbed aboard the ship. The man boldly snatched up a chisel and tongs from the deck, jumped overboard, and swam toward a waiting canoe. Clerke ordered his men to open fire on the swimmer, but they missed. The master of the *Discovery* Thomas Edgar, Midshipman George Vancouver, and two other sailors quickly rowed a boat in pursuit of the thief. On shore, Captain Cook learned of the theft and began dashing from one group of natives to another, angrily demanding the return of the stolen goods. Shaken by these violent reactions, the Hawaiians returned the tools.

Master Edgar, however, refused to let the matter drop. Vengefully he decided to seize Parea's canoe and hold it until the thief was turned over. Parea, now back on shore, tried to protect his property. Other shouting natives crowded around the sailors and an ugly scuffle erupted. Parea grabbed Edgar, but a seaman struck the chief with an oar and knocked him to the ground. As the British swam into the water in retreat, the Hawaiians picked up stones and pelted them. Luckily, as the violence mounted, Parea began to realize that things had gone too far. He restored order and asked forgiveness of the British.

Captain Cook grew furious when he learned of this unfortunate brawl. His sailors might have handled the problem in a much more peaceful manner. He now realized, though, that bad feelings among the Hawaiians posed a growing threat. "I am afraid," he declared, "that these people will oblige me to use some violent measures, for they must not be left to imagine they have gained an advantage over us."

That night, natives swam out to the *Discovery* and boldly stole one of the ship's boats that was anchored in the water. The theft of that boat set in motion a tragic chain of events. Stationed on shore with the men repairing the mast, Lieutenant King learned of the missing boat the next morning as he rowed out to the *Resolution*. "When I arrived on board," he later recalled, "I found the marines arming, and Captain Cook loading his double-barreled gun."

Cook ordered King to take his boat crew to the far end of the bay and block any action by the natives there. At the same time, Cook planned to row to shore with Lieutenant Molesworth Phillips and nine marines aboard the *Resolution*'s two boats. Cook's practice of holding a native chief hostage until stolen items were returned had always worked before. Now he angrily expected to get the *Discovery*'s boat back by the same method.

Shortly after seven o'clock on the morning of February 14, 1779, Cook and his party reached the beach. With the armed marines marching behind them, Cook and Phillips strode into the sleepy native village and halted before one of the larger huts. Stepping inside, Lieutenant Phillips awakened Kalaniopu'u, the leading chieftain of the bay. He told the old man that Captain Cook had come to visit him. Outside, Cook invited the chief aboard the *Resolution*. Apparently unaware of the growing tensions, Kalaniopu'u willingly agreed.

As the group began walking toward the beach, Kalaniopu'u's wife ran down from the village crying loudly. Two younger chiefs also hurried close. They suspected their leader was in danger and insisted Kalaniopu'u sit down in the sand and not go one step further. At every moment, more worried and angry Hawaiians crowded onto the beach. Scowling Hawaiians jostled the marines as the enormous mob surged close.

Just then, a canoe sped up to the beach. An excited native burst through the crowd with word that the British at the far end of the bay had killed a favorite chief. Fearlessly Cook permitted his men to fall back and take up positions near the shoreline. Slowly and calmly, Cook and Phillips edged their way through the pressing throng. With their backs to the sea, they and the nine marines anxiously kept their muskets at the ready.

The natives shouted among themselves. Some men had put on their war cloaks of thickly woven palm leaves. Others fiercely shook their clubs and spears, while many picked up stones. In the midst of this angry mob, Cook realized his serious danger.

Enraged by news of the murdered chief, one Hawaiian warrior lunged at Cook with his dagger. Cook felt he must protect himself. One barrel of his musket was filled with small shot usually used to kill birds. The other barrel was loaded with a solid lead ball. Cook fired the small shot at the man, but because of the thick matting of the native's war cloak, it had no effect.

Boldly the Hawaiians now advanced, hurling stones at the line of marines. A chief stabbed Lieutenant Phillips in the shoulder with a spear. Another native knocked a marine to the ground. Backing toward the beach, Cook fired his second barrel, killing one attacking Hawaiian. Dreadful shouts rose up from the crowd. Cook called upon the marines to fire. The whistling volley of bullets stunned the mob for a moment, and the British hurried to reload their muskets.

"Take to the boats!" shouted Cook.

Frantically the marines scrambled into the shallow water as the Hawaiians wildly charged around them. Standing behind on the beach, Captain Cook waved for the sailors in the boats to pull closer to the shore. In another moment he might have waded out to safety. But already he was surrounded and it was too late. A native struck him with a staggering blow from behind with a club. Another stabbed him repeatedly with a dagger. He dropped face-down into the water. The surprised natives saw Cook's bloody wound and realized in an instant that he was no god. With mad fury they crowded over his fallen body, stabbing him again and again with daggers and spears.

The bloody fight ended soon afterwards. The bodies of four marines also lay among the rocks along the shoreline. Roaring, four-pound cannon on the *Resolution* cleared the natives from the beach, as the survivors of the battle silently rowed back and boarded the ship. The sad news they brought stunned every British sailor. Captain Cook was dead. During a dreadful hour of misunderstanding and confusion, the great explorer had fallen. "We all felt we had lost a father," one grieving sailor later declared.

Scene just before the tragic death of James Cook

According to rank, Lieutenant Clerke took command of the expedition. During the next hours, fearful crewmen watched the shore, prepared to fight if necessary. An uneasy peace slowly settled over the bay. Both the British and the Hawaiians came to realize that tragic mistakes had led to Cook's death.

Lieutenant Clerke demanded the return of his captain's body. He soon learned that the Hawaiians had cut it up according to their custom. On a wooden pyre they had burned the corpse in a funeral ritual reserved for only the highest chiefs. Five days after Cook's death, a mournful native priest approached the *Resolution*. He handed over to Lieutenant Clerke a handsome bundled cloak of black and white feathers. Wrapped inside lay some of Captain Cook's blackened bones.

Clerke placed these remains in a coffin. At sunset on February 21, ten cannon aboard the *Resolution* boomed in solemn salute. Flags and pennants fluttered at half staff. Dressed in their best uniforms, officers and crewmen stood at sad attention while one of the officers read from Captain Cook's Bible. Then the sailors lowered the coffin into the lapping waters of the bay.

The repairs aboard the *Resolution* were finished. On the gray, rainy evening of February 23, both the *Resolution* and the *Discovery* set sail and left Kealakekua Bay behind. It was Lieutenant Clerke's difficult task to complete Cook's voyage. He appointed Lieutenant John Gore to command the *Discovery*, while he stayed aboard the *Resolution*.

Kealakekua Bay today

The ships sailed northwest toward the Asian mainland, and in April they skirted along the Russian peninsula of Kamchatka. At a coastal trading village called St. Peter and St. Paul, the British stopped for supplies. Clerke penned a letter to the British Admiralty, and it began its long land journey across the Russian frontier. Despite the great distance, the letter reached home. The English learned the sad news of Cook's death a full eight months before the voyage ended.

From Kamchatka, Clerke relentlessly steered north to make another sweep into the Arctic. For weeks the ships slowly picked their way through floating ice and blinding fogs. By the end of July, they had sailed as far as they could go. Fifteen miles (twenty-four kilometers) short of the farthest advance of the previous year, a great wall of ice twenty feet (six meters) high now stood. It would be useless to keep the weather-beaten ships in this frozen wasteland any longer. Clerke turned back on July 27. "We were all heartily sick of navigation full of danger," admitted Lieutenant King.

Clerke had been in poor health with tuberculosis from the very start of the voyage. On August 22, 1779, during the journey south, the gallant young officer finally died of that disease. Following Clerke's burial on Kamchatka, the *Resolution* and the *Discovery* started homeward under the overall command of Lieutenant Gore.

Months of hard travel lay ahead. The long, difficult trip included stops for supplies and repairs along the coast of China, passage through the Java Sea, and another stop at Cape Town, on Africa's tip. In spite of the war raging between Great Britain and the United

Gore returned his ship to England with the help of this famous chronometer, which Cook took on his second and third voyages. Designed by Larcum Kendall in 1769, it was a copy of John Harrison's prize-winning chronometer.

States and France, the *Resolution* and the *Discovery* sailed north across the Atlantic Ocean without danger of attack. The United States and France had granted the two ships free passage out of respect for Captain Cook. For added safety, Lieutenant Gore guided the vessels north around Ireland and Scotland instead of approaching the French coast. At long last, they passed along the eastern coast of England, and on October 4, 1780, the *Resolution* and the *Discovery* entered the Thames River after a voyage of four years, two months, and twenty-two days.

The British people expressed little joy over the return of the two ships. The tragedy of Captain Cook's death remained too fresh in their minds. "His name will live forever," Sir Joseph Banks mournfully told Cook's widow. With quiet strength and fearless determination, James Cook had left his nation and the world a giant legacy.

"In every situation," Seaman David Samwell respectfully remembered, "he stood unrivalled and alone; on him all eyes were turned: he was our leading star."

During his three long voyages Cook had covered wider distances, seen more strange lands and cultures, and brought back a greater knowledge of the earth than any navigator before or since. He destroyed the myths of a southern continent and a northern passage and drew instead the first true map of the vast Pacific Ocean.

"No man who used the Sea could tell where he would be buried," Cook once wrote in his journal. Though he died in Hawaiian waters far from home, surely James Cook's spirit still survives in the names of his four ships: *Endeavour*, *Resolution*, *Adventure*, and *Discovery*.

Captain James Cook, 1728-1779

Appendices

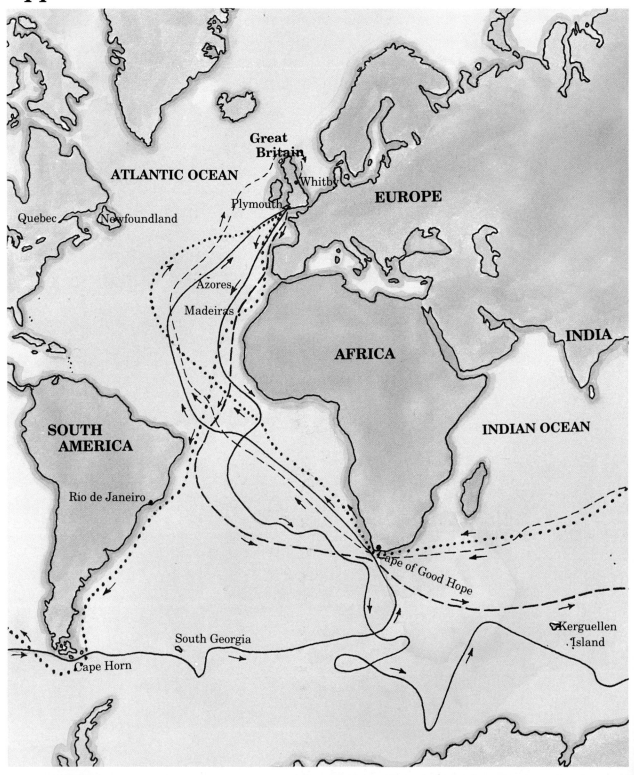

ATLANTIC OCEAN

Great Britain

Whitby

EUROPE

Quebec

Newfoundland

Plymouth

Azores

Madeiras

AFRICA

INDIA

SOUTH AMERICA

INDIAN OCEAN

Rio de Janeiro

Cape of Good Hope

South Georgia

Kerguellen Island

Cape Horn

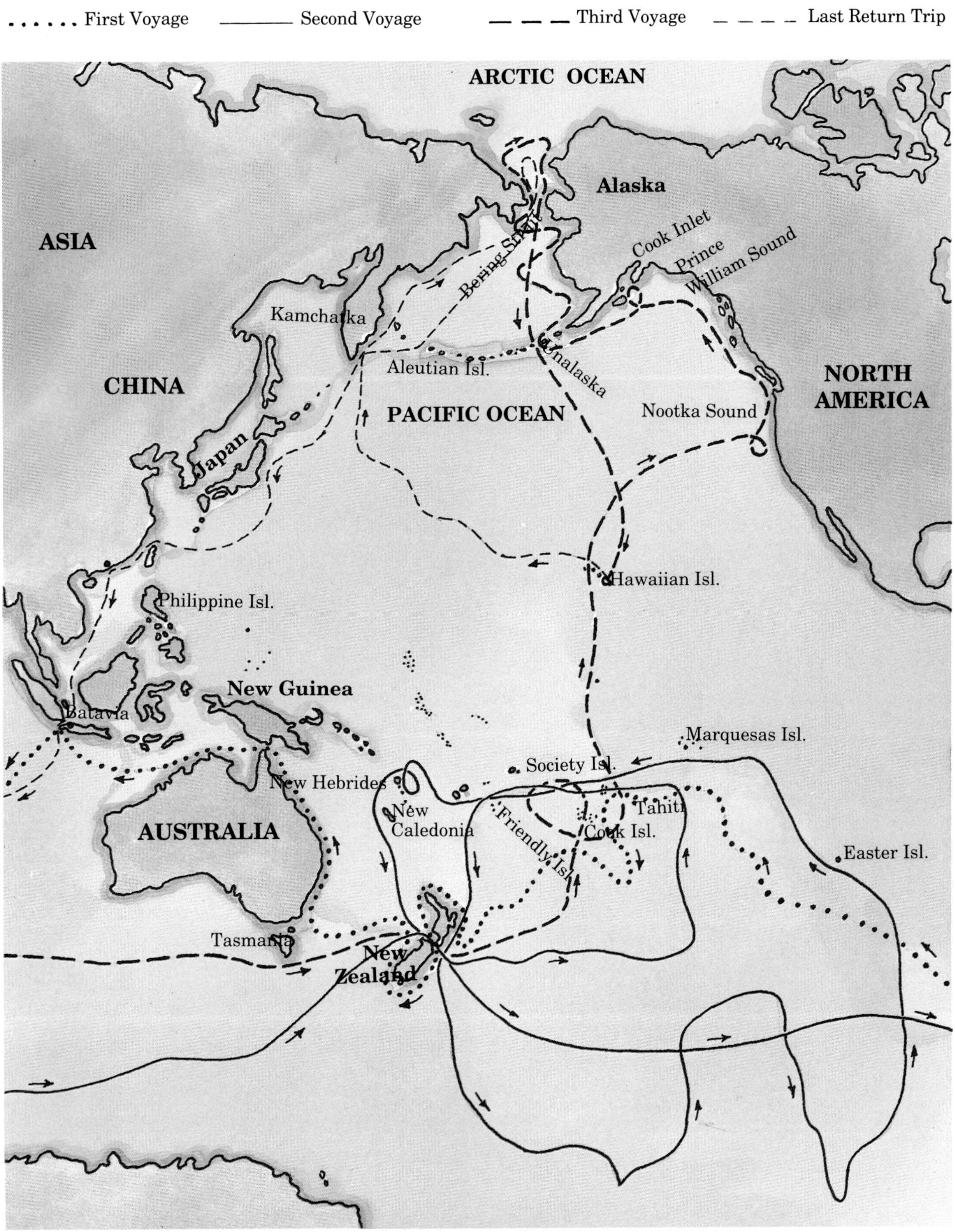

····· First Voyage ——— Second Voyage — — — Third Voyage — — — Last Return Trip

ARCTIC OCEAN

Alaska

ASIA

Cook Inlet

Prince
William Sound

Kamchatka

Bering Strait

Aleutian Isl.

Unalaska

CHINA

PACIFIC OCEAN

NORTH
AMERICA

Nootka Sound

Japan

Hawaiian Isl.

Philippine Isl.

New Guinea

Marquesas Isl.

Batavia

Society Isl.

New Hebrides

Tahiti

New
Caledonia

Friendly Isl.

Cook Isl.

Easter Isl.

AUSTRALIA

Tasmania

New
Zealand

Australian Wildlife

Young dingoes

Wombat

Tree kangaroo

Tasmanian devil

Colorful sea life on
the Great Barrier Reef

Sea anemones on
the Great Barrier Reef

Koala eating eucalyptus leaves

Wallaby

Timeline of Events in Cook's Lifetime

1728 —James Cook is born on October 27 in the village of Marton-in-Cleveland, England

1735 —John Harrison invents the chronometer, an instrument that keeps accurate time at sea

1736 —The Cooks move to Ayton, where James is enrolled in Postgate School

1740 —James goes to work as an apprentice in William Sanderson's general store in the town of Staithes

1746 —James goes to Whitby to work as an apprentice seaman for John and Henry Walker on a type of coalship known as a Whitby Cat

1755 —Cook is made captain of the coalship *Friendship*; he signs up as an able seaman for the British Royal Navy; he is promoted to master's mate, or assistant navigator, and then to boatswain

1756 —Under the command of Captain Hugh Palliser, Cook engages in a sea battle aboard HMS *Eagle*; Palliser promotes him to ship's mate, or navigator

1758 —As navigator on HMS *Pembroke*, Cook charts the St. Lawrence River near Quebec, aiding in the British victory over the French at Quebec

1761 — Cook returns to England and marries Elizabeth Batts

1763-1767 —Cook surveys the coasts of Newfoundland and Labrador; an exploding powder horn severely injures his hand in 1764

1768 — Aboard HMS *Endeavour*, Cook embarks on his first expedition to the South Pacific

1769 —With astronomer Charles Green, Cook observes the Transit of Venus from Tahiti; he explores along New Zealand's coast

1770 — Cook establishes that New Zealand consists of two islands; while exploring Australia's eastern coast, his ship is badly damaged on the Great Barrier Reef

1771 — Cook returns to England and is promoted to commander

1772 — Cook embarks on his second voyage, taking HMS *Adventure* and HMS *Resolution* on an expedition into the South Atlantic, South Indian, and South Pacific oceans and the waters around Antarctica

1774 — HMS *Adventure*'s Captain Tobias Furneaux returns to England, becoming the first to circle the globe following a west-to-east route

1775 — Cook and his crew on HMS *Resolution* return to England; he is promoted to post-captain and appointed captain of the Royal Hospital for Seamen

1776 — With HMS *Resolution* and *Discovery*, Cook leaves on his third voyage; among his duties is to look for the Northwest Passage, a northern sea route between the Atlantic and Pacific oceans

1778 — Cook explores along the coast of Alaska until stopped by ice in the Arctic Ocean; he decides to go to the Sandwich Islands (Hawaii) for the winter

1779 — Cook's fleet sails into Hawaii's Kealakekua Bay in January; he leaves but is forced by a storm to return to the bay; the crew engage in conflicts with natives, during which James Cook is killed on February 14; Lieutenant Charles Clerke, commander of the *Discovery*, takes charge of the expedition, but dies of tuberculosis on August 22; John Gore, first lieutenant aboard the *Resolution*, then takes charge, returning to England in 1780

Glossary of Terms

able seaman—A trained seaman who is able to perform a number of shipboard duties

aborigines—The original native people of a region, rather than later settlers; commonly refers to Australia's native people

apprentice—One who learns a trade by working under a master

boatswain—A ship's officer who is in charge of shipboard maintenance and repairs

capstan—A rotating vertical shaft around which cables are wound for lifting or hauling

caulk—To fill seams with a sealing material

chandler—A merchant who provides supplies for a specific purpose, such as a sailing expedition

constellation—A group of stars that appear to outline a certain pattern

continent—One of the seven great land masses on the earth

flagship—The ship on which a fleet's captain sails

hemisphere—A half of the earth's surface; the earth is usually divided into its northern and southern hemispheres or its eastern and western hemispheres.

HMS—His (or Her) Majesty's Ship; used with ships' names to designate vessels in Great Britain's Royal Navy

isthmus—A narrow strip of land between two bodies of water

landfall—The first point of land sighted during an ocean voyage

leadsman—A ship's crewman who lowers lead weights into the water to measure its depth

mizzenmast—The mast just behind a ship's main mast

oakum—Long plant fibers soaked with tar; used to fill seams in ships' hulls

quadrant—A navigational instrument that measures the angle of elevation of the sun, the moon, or a star

scurvy—A disease, once common among sailors, caused by lack of vitamin C

theodolite—A surveying instrument that measures angles

trade wind—A wind over a particular area of the ocean that always blows in a certain direction

troopship—A ship that carries military troops

Bibliography

For further reading, see:

Beaglehole, John Cawte. *The Life of Captain James Cook*. Stanford, CA: Stanford University Press, 1974.

Conner, Daniel, and Miller, Lorraine. *Master Mariner, Capt. James Cook and the People of the Pacific*. Vancouver, BC: Douglas & McIntyre, 1978.

The Explorations of Captain James Cook in the Pacific as Told by Selections of His Own Journals 1768-1779. A. Grenfill Price, editor. Sydney, Australia: Angus and Robertson, 1969.

MacLean, Alistair. *Captain Cook*. Garden City, NY: Doubleday, 1972.

Villiers, Alan John. *Captain James Cook*. NY: Charles Scribner's, 1967.

Warner, Oliver, and the editors of Horizon Magazine. *Captain Cook and the South Pacific*. NY: American Heritage Publishing Co., 1963.

Index

Page numbers in boldface type indicate illustrations.

Picture Identifications for Chapter Opening Spreads

6-7—Cook with his ships in Kealakekua Bay, Hawaii
12-13—Island in the St. Lawrence River near Quebec
22-23—The dockyard at Deptford, England
32-33—Tahiti: scene from the top of the island
46-47—Eastern gray kangaroo, Queensland, Australia
58-59—Pack ice of Antarctica
70-71—King penguins on South Georgia Island in the South Atlantic
80-81—Tasman Sea as seen from South Tasmania
92-93—Sunset at Kauai, Hawaii
102-103—Kauai beach at dawn

Picture Acknowledgments

The Bettmann Archive—21, 40, 62, 82 (top), 91, 105, 115

Cameramann International, Ltd.—38 (bottom), 39, 112, 119 (bottom left)

Gartman Agency: © James P. Rowan—44; © David Seman—32-33, 38 (margin), 67

© **Virginia R. Grimes**—5, 119 (top left, top right)

Historical Pictures Service, Chicago—9, 15, 20, 24, 29, 42, 79, 82 (margin), 84, 95, 99

© **Emilie Lepthien**—70-71, 77

Len Meents—Map on 116-117

National Maritime Museum, Greenwich, England—45, 61, 65, 114

North Wind Picture Archives—2, 6-7, 10, 11, 16, 19, 22-23, 26, 35, 37, 43, 53, 55, 69, 73, 85, 90, 106, 111

Odyssey Productions: © Robert Frerck—48, 51, 80-81, 118 (top right, bottom left, bottom right)

R/C Photo Agency: © Richard L. Capps—4

© **Bob & Ira Spring**—76 (2 pictures), 86

Tom Stack & Associates: © Rich Buzzelli—49; © J. Cancalosi—119 (bottom right); © Manfred Gottschalk—54; © Stewart M. Green—88; © Jack S. Grove—58-59, 64, 74; © Ann and Myron Sutton—118 (top left)

Tony Stone Worldwide Chicago, Ltd.: © Cliff Hollenbeck—92-93

Valan: © John Cancalosi—46-47, 52; © Kennon Cooke—12-13; © A. Farquhar—102-103; © Johnny Johnson—97; © Stephen J. Krasemann—101

About the Author

Zachary Kent grew up in Little Falls, New Jersey, and received an English degree from St. Lawrence University. After college he worked at a New York City literary agency for two years before launching his writing career. To support himself while writing, he has worked as a taxi driver, a shipping clerk, and a house painter. Mr. Kent has had a lifelong interest in history, especially American history. Studying the U.S. presidents was his childhood hobby. His collection of presidential items includes books, pictures, and games, as well as several autographed letters.